Markets

Colin Bamford and Stephen Munday

Series Editor
Susan Grant
West Oxfordshire College

Heinemann

Colin Bamford would like to thank Karen Brooke for word-processing the original manuscript and Sue Grant for her inspiration and comments throughout. Finally and not least I would like to thank my wife Elisabeth and daughters Emily and Alice for allowing me the time to write. I hope I have not neglected them in the process.

Heinemann Educational Publishers
Halley Court, Jordan Hill, Oxford, OX2 8EJ
a division of Reed Educational & Professional Publishing Ltd.

Heinemann is a registered trademark of Reed Educational and
Professional Publishing Ltd.

OXFORD MELBOURNE AUCKLAND
JOHANNESBURG BLANTYRE GABORONE
IBADAN PORTSMOUTH NH (USA) CHICAGO

Text © Colin Bamford and Stephen Munday 2002
First published in 2002

06 05 04 03 02
9 8 7 6 5 4 3 2 1

British Library Cataloguing in Publication Data
A catalogue record for this book is available from the British Library

ISBN 0 435 33223 6

Typeset and illustrated by Techtype, Abingdon, Oxon
Printed and bound in Great Britain by Biddles Ltd, Guildford

Acknowledgements
The authors and publishers would like to thank the following for the use of copyright material:

AQA for the question on p. 74 © AQA examination questions are reproduced by permission of the Assessment and Qualifications Alliance; The Mitre Corporation Center for Advanced Aviation System for the extract on p. 13; The Christchurch Press for the extract on p. 50 © The Press, Christchurch; the *Daily Mail* for the extract on p. 110 © the *Daily Mail*; The Economist for the extract on p. 28 © The Economist Newspaper Limited, London, June 30th 2001; Edexcel for the questions on p. 23, 44, 59, 102 and 117 © Edexcel; the *Evening Standard* for the extract on p. 84 © *Evening Standard*; the *Financial Times* for the extracts on p. 69 © Financial Times, 27/3/02 and p. 74 © Financial Times, 22/2/00 and the graph on p. 74 © Financial Times, 8/2/00; *The Guardian* for the extract on p. 4 © The Guardian; *The Independent* for the extract on p. 5 © Extracted from an article by John Lichfield, first published in *The Independent* 1 January 2002 and the extract on p. 51 © Extracted from an article by Charles Arthur, first published in *The Independent* 18 June 2002 and the extract on p. 57 © Extracted from an article by William Kay, first published in *The Independent* 9 March 2002; The Institute of Grocery Distribution for the table on p. 108; the *Nursing Times* for the extract on p. 84 reproduced by kind permission of Nursing Times where this first appeared in the article *UK still targeting Third World* by Craig Kenny, Volume 97, No 33, 16-22 August 2001, p.5; OCR for the questions on p. 43, 44, 73 and 116 reproduced with the kind permission of OCR; ONS for the graphs on p. 38 and the table on p. 95 © Crown Copyright material is reproduced under Class Licence Number C01W00141 with the permission of the Controller of HMSO and the Queen's Printer for Scotland; *The Observer* for the extract on p. 22 © The Observer; *The Sunday Times (Singapore)* for the extract on p. 90 © Adapted from 'It's a bargain hunters paradise in Japan' *The Sunday Times (Singapore)* 3 June 2001; *The Daily Telegraph* for the articles on p. 6 (26/5/02), p. 14 (12/12/01), p. 16 (2/02/00), p. 17 (14/4/01), p. 48 (11/08/01), p. 67 (12/5/02), p. 70 (14/12/00), p. 72 (14/01/01), p. 80 (28/12/01), p. 84 (15/08/98), p. 100 (25/01/02), p. 110 (05/01/02), p. 115 (11/03/00) © Telegraph Group Limited; *The Times* for the extract on p. 102 (5/1/00) and p. 111 (18/09/01) © Times newspapers Limited, London.

The publishers have made every effort to trace the copyright holders, but if they have inadvertently overlooked any, they will be pleased to make the necessary arrangements at the first opportunity.

Tel: 01865 888058 www.heinemann.co.uk

Contents

Websites
Links to appropriate websites are given throughout the book/pack. Although these were up to date at the time of writing, it is essential for teachers to preview these sites before using them with pupils. This will ensure that the web address (URL) is still accurate and the content is suitable for your needs.

We suggest that you bookmark useful sites and consider enabling pupils to access them through the school intranet. We are bringing this to your attention, as we are aware of legitimate sites being appropriated illegally by people wanting to distribute unsuitable or offensive material. We strongly advise you to purchase suitable screening software so that pupils are protected from unsuitable sites and their material.

If you do find that the links given no longer work, or the content is unsuitable, please let us know. Details of changes will be posted on our website.

Preface

Colin Bamford and Stephen Munday are two well-known authors and prominent examiners. In this new book they explore the most fundamental aspect of economics – the operation of markets. Throughout, their approach is to elucidate theory by reference to real world markets.

The book is an excellent introduction to the study of markets for AS/A level students and for undergraduates who might be studying economics for the first time. It should prove to be particularly useful for students studying AQA's AS module 1, Edexcel's AS unit 1, and OCR's module 2881.

Susan Grant
Series Editor

Introduction

Students of Economics in the twenty-first century might understandably find difficulty in comprehending what life was like at the end of the eighteenth century. In the ever-shrinking world of today's global economy, where affluent consumers demand the latest technology and devices, it may come as a surprise for students to learn that much of the economic theory in this book has it origins in the work of Adam Smith, the founder of classical economics, who wrote his master-work, *The Wealth of Nations*, well over two hundred years ago.

Market economics, and Smith's 'invisible hand', have come back into fashion, demonstrating their strong intellectual and dialectical appeal. Throughout the world, in most rich as well as in many poor countries, the key role markets can play in economic systems is increasingly being appreciated. This book demonstrates why that is so, using up-to-date applications drawn from a wide range of real market situations.

Chapter One looks at the nature of markets. It shows why the operation of markets is at the core of economics and how, despite the many types of market and sub-markets, all markets have the common characteristic of existing where buyers and sellers, consumers and producers, meet to trade and exchange goods and services.

Chapters Two and *Three* focus on the demand side of markets. *Chapter Two* explains what economists mean by demand, and the fundamental conceptual relationship that exists between demand and price in any type of market. It also considers the other factors that need to be incorporated to give a full explanation of the determinants of demand. *Chapter Three* concentrates on the important concept of elasticities of demand. As well as what these measures mean in theory, the chapter stresses their business significance and relevance to decision-makers.

Chapter Four concentrates on the supply side. It follows a similar format to *Chapters Two* and *Three*, in considering the relationship between supply and prices, the other influences on supply, and the factors that can affect the price elasticity of supply of a product.

In *Chapter Five*, the demand and supply sides of markets are brought together through an analysis of price determination and equilibrium in markets. It also explains how the market equilibrium can change as a consequence of changes in demand and supply.

Chapter Six presents a wide range of examples of markets in action. It covers the workings of the labour, money, foreign exchange, housing and agricultural markets. The theoretical underpinning is drawn from earlier chapters, and for each market, recent stimulus material is provided to show its relevance.

Chapter Seven links the analysis of markets to the way in which markets are organized. Again, through relevant examples, it demonstrates how the power of the market can be affected by market structures, and why – in practice – markets do not always work as freely as the theory suggests because of the concentration of control in the hands of a small number of producers.

Chapter One

The nature of markets

'The key insight of Adam Smith's The Wealth of Nations *is misleadingly simple: If an exchange between two parties is voluntary, it will not take place unless both believe that they will benefit from it.'*
Milton Friedman.

The subject of economics

- Why can we not have everything that we want?
- Should we use more resources for education and less for something else?
- Who should receive what, in our local area, in our country, in our world?

These are all questions of economics. They all stem from the fundamental problem that lies at the heart of the study of the subject of economics. On the one hand, there is no limit to what we might desire: we have **infinite wants**. On the other hand, there is a clear limit to what we have available for meeting those wants: we have **scarce resources**. These resources are categorized in four ways by economists:

- **land** – all natural resources
- **labour** – all human effort available for production
- **capital** – all human-made forms of production
- **enterprise** – the human force that puts all the other factors of production to work.

This is the essence of the subject of economics: how do we reconcile this fundamental problem of our human existence?

This problem means that **economic choices** have to be made. Everything is not possible, so we must decide what to do. In particular, every society has to make three particular choices about what to do with its scarce resources:

- What should it produce?
- How should it produce it?
- For whom should it produce?

There have to be ways to answer these vital questions if any economy is to function at all.

Answering the fundamental questions

Every society has to work out how it will answer the fundamental questions. It has to find the best way to try to resolve the economic problem. It must find a way to allocate its scarce resources in order best to meet its infinite wants. There are really two ways of going about this:

- The government can make all the decisions. The government of a country can decide what products to make and what resources should be used to make them. It can decide how things should be made and who should get them.
- Markets can be allowed to determine the process. Markets for resources and for goods and services can be allowed to operate freely. They will lead to resources being allocated to the production of particular products. Markets can determine how the products will be made and who will receive them.

In practice, it is possible for societies to have some decisions made by the government and others made by markets. This is the case in virtually every country in the world.

The purpose of this book is to examine markets. It will look at what markets are and how they operate. It will show how market forces cause scarce resources to be allocated towards our infinite wants. As

Shoppers deal retailers a seasonal high

JILL TREANOR

As Victoria Beckham led the charge for the 'posh' shoppers at the start of yesterday's Harrod's sale, the stock market was pinning its hopes on purchases made by more ordinary shoppers in middle-market high-street stores during the festive period.

While the trading statements from the listed retailers – from clothing to electricals – continue to be prepared, City dealers were left to rely on more anecdotal evidence about healthy Christmas sales yesterday.

The City seems convinced that the apparently liberal use of credit cards in the run-up to Christmas is good news for the retailers, and share prices in many of the big retail names yesterday continued the rise which began at the end of last year.

The Guardian, 3 January 2002

such, it investigates a fundamental part of the subject of economics.

What is a market?
If we are to study markets, we need to be clear what they are. We could all name many markets. Two important markets are referred to in *The Guardian* article about shopping. These are:

* the **stock market** – this is the market for shares in companies
* the **retail market** – this is a wide-ranging market that embraces virtually all **consumer products**.

Markets could also represent a geographical area. The article from *The Independent* about the birth of the **euro** refers to an important geographical market – the so-called **single market** in Europe. This is

At last, the euro is born

JOHN LICHFIELD

For the first time in almost 2000 years, Europe – or a large part of it – has a single currency. From Prussia to County Kerry, from Lapland to Crete, 300 million people are paying for their daily bread or their daily newspaper using the same kind of banknotes and, with slight artistic variations, the same kind of coins.

World-transforming events sometimes happen without us noticing them. Who remembers the precise moment the microchip was invented? Or the Internet? Overnight, there occurred a piece of slow-motion history, programmed ten years in advance. Twelve countries gave up their national currencies – part of their identity, part of their sovereignty, part of their ability to control their own economic and political destiny – voluntarily.

Economists argue that the true, historical moment occurred three years ago, when twelve national currencies were permanently fixed against each other. With this came the true completion of the Single Market in Europe where prices could no longer fluctuate between those countries due to changes in the exchange rate. One of the final barriers to free trade was removed between the twelve countries.

However, the real moment of importance was the creation and use of euro currency. The euro was created for political reasons, not for economic ones. After the collapse of the Soviet bloc, a single European currency was willed by the French government, conceded by the Germans and accepted by the others – but not by the British – as a counterweight to German reunification and the inevitable expansion of the EU to the east. The economic arguments, sound though they may be, were tagged on later.

The Independent, 1 January 2002

another important example of a market. Economists argue that the single currency strengthens the single market. The author of the article thinks that the implications are more political than this.

Another very important market in the United Kingdom that has a significant impact on many people's lives is the housing market. The major market players are estate agents. They make the market move as they have the key role of bringing together buyers and sellers. The article below about estate agents indicates an area of the market that they might wish to activate further.

What is it that makes all of these examples, and any others, 'markets'? What is the essence of a market? The answer is the same for all markets:

- A market is any place or mechanism through which **buyers** and **sellers** meet in order to **trade**.
- Markets exist when **consumers** and **producers** come together in order to exchange goods and services.
- A market can thus be a physical place where any product is bought and sold. However, it need not be a physical place. The telephone is

Estate Agents drool over bishop's palaces

JONATHAN PETRE

Each would make you the envy of your neighbours. A clutch of bishops' palaces and houses, some dating back centuries and boasting private chapels, are set to come on to the market under a cost-cutting review by the Church Commissioners.

The average bishops' house is worth £550,000 and values range from about £350,000 to more than £2 million.

Apart from Lambeth Palace and Bishopsthorpe, the seat of the Archbishop of York, one of the grandest houses is Auckland Castle, the seat of the Bishop of Durham since the twelfth century.

Stuart Edwards, an estate agent in Durham, said the castle would be worth around £2 million.

'There is potential to convert it into smaller dwellings. In Weir Valley there are some nice properties, and there was one recently for £750,000 but generally speaking there is not much in excess of £500,000 in the area. I'd be delighted to have it on my books. I am sure that I could find buyers'.

The present bishop, the Rt Rev Michael Turnbull, lives in a four-bedroom apartment in the castle, which is set in six acres of garden surrounded by a 400-acre park.

The Daily Telegraph, 26 May 2002

a market mechanism as it provides a means by which buyers and sellers are brought into contact. The Internet is another major market mechanism. Virtually anything can now be bought and sold via the Internet. Any such activity represents a market.

What do markets do?

Markets can be seen as absolutely central to the operation of any economy. They allow producers to sell their products. They allow consumers to buy the products that they wish to and are able to purchase. In this sense, they facilitate the whole working of the economic system. The two key economic groups are brought together through markets in order to participate in a key economic activity – trade.

Markets are thus at the heart of the resolution of the **fundamental economic problem**. They provide the means through which scarce resources satisfy consumer wants. Scarce resources are turned into products by producers. These are then sold to consumers through markets. These products are what bring the satisfaction of wants.

Central to the functioning of markets is *price*. Every market for a product is associated with a price. Sellers are able to sell their product at a certain price. Buyers can buy the product at a certain price. The **market price** is central to the operation of markets. Much of the purpose of this book is to consider how that market price is determined in every market. How does the interaction of suppliers and consumers cause a price to be created in markets?

The final point to note here about markets is that it can be suggested that they may not only achieve the allocation of scarce resources to meet infinite wants. They may also do that job *well*. If we assume that producers make products from scarce resources in order to make profits, then two things follow:

• Producers must make goods and services that consumers are willing and able to purchase. They must bring products to a market that will sell. Only in this way can profit be made. Through this simple process, markets ensure that the right products are made – those that do most to satisfy wants.
• Producers will produce products as cheaply as possible. In other words, they will use as few scarce resources as possible. This allows producers to sell goods and services at as low a price as possible. They are thus able to sell as many products as possible.

Markets can thus allow the right products to be produced using as few scarce resources as possible. Economists refer to this as **efficiency**.

```
                        KEY WORDS

Infinite wants              Single market
Scarce resources            Buyers
Land                        Sellers
Labour                      Trade
Capital                     Consumers
Enterprise                  Producers
Economic choices            Fundamental economic
Stock market                   problem
Retail market               Market price
Consumer products           Efficiency
Euro
```

Further reading
Anderton, A., Unit 15 in *Economics*, 3rd edn, Causeway Press, 2000.
Bamford, C. (ed.), Unit 1, section 1 in *Economics for AS*, Cambridge University Press, 2000.
Bamford, C. (ed.), Unit 1 in *Economics AS Level and A Level*, Cambridge University Press, 2002.
Munday, S., Chapter 1 in *Markets and Market Failure*, Heinemann Educational, 2000.

Useful website
Retail sales: www.statistics.gov.uk
Click on Economy; click on short term indicators.

Essay topics
1. Using examples, define what economists mean by the term 'market'.
   [10 marks]

2. Explain and comment upon the way in which the functioning of markets helps to resolve the fundamental economic problem.
   [15 marks]

Data response question
The following questions refer to the article 'At last the euro is born' on page 5.

1. (a) Define the term 'market'. [2 marks]
   (b) Explain how much of Europe operates as a market. [4 marks]

2. Explain how the introduction of the euro removes 'one of the final barriers to free trade' in the European Single Market. [6 marks]

3. Discuss the suggestion that the real reason for the introduction of the single currency in Europe is not to do with economic arguments in favour of such a development. [8 marks]

Chapter Two

Demand

*'Regard to our own private happiness and interest, too, appear upon
many occasions very laudable principles of action.'*
Adam Smith, *The Theory of Moral Sentiments.*

Wants and demand

If the fundamental economic problem is to be tackled, then people's
wants have to be satisfied. **Demand** looks at what consumers want.
However, consumer demand goes beyond just consumer wants. There
is a crucial difference between a want and demand:

* A want is anything at all that may be desired by a consumer. There
  is no limit to this. A consumer is willing to consume virtually every
  consumer product that may exist.
* For demand to exist, consumers must be not only *willing* to
  purchase and consume a product; they must also be *able* to do so.

The difference between a want and a demand for a product is the
ability to pay. Demanding goes further than wanting. Demand is a
want that is backed up with resources to purchase the product. In our
modern monetary societies, the simplest way of putting it is: *Demand is
a want backed by money.*

Economists sometimes express this distinction between wants and
demand in a different fashion. They refer to **notional demand** and
effective demand:

* Notional demand represents everything that consumers could
  possibly ask for. In other words, it is the same thing as consumer
  wants.
* Effective demand represents only that demand that is backed up by
  the ability to purchase a product.

Producers are interested only in effective demand. In a market, it is only
demand or effective demand that is really meaningful. Producers will
try to meet demand in order to make profits.

A full definition of demand

Having established the crucial difference between wants and demand, a
full definition of the economic concept of demand can be given.

Demand is defined as the amount (or quantity) of a product that consumers are willing and able to purchase at various prices over a given time period.

Certain points need to be noted about this definition in addition to the distinction between wants and demand:

- Demand for a product will be different at different prices. This is a fundamental rule in economics that will be investigated later in this chapter.
- It is necessary to specify the period of time that is being considered. The amount of demand for a product will be different in an hour to that in a day or in a year.
- It must also be assumed that other things are not changing when looking at the relationship between the amount demanded and the price of the product. Economists refer to this as *ceteris paribus* – which means 'other things being equal'. Nothing else must be changing if the effect of just price is to be seen.

The relationship between price and demand

It has been noted that the relationship between the price of a product and the quantity demanded of that product is a central one in economics. A strong assumption is made. It is an assumption that is deemed virtually always to be the case. It is referred to as the **law of demand**. This law states:

There is an inverse relationship between the price of a product and the amount of demand for a product. The higher the price, the lower the demand. The lower the price, the higher the demand.

This law rests on two crucial assumptions about how consumers behave:

- Consumers are **rational**, in that they make decisions based on rational decision-making. If the identical product is available at two different prices, the consumer will opt for the product at the lower price.
- Consumers aim to satisfy their wants as fully as possible. This attempt to satisfy wants is often referred to as **utility**. Consumers will purchase the bundle of products that best satisfies their consumer wants.

Given these two assumptions, there are several reasons given as to why there will be an inverse relationship between price and the quantity demanded:

- The lower the price of a product, the more a consumer can afford. This becomes especially true with products that take up a significant percentage of a consumer's budget. Economists refer to this as the **income effect**.
- The lower the price of a product, the better value that product becomes compared to any possible alternative products (or **substitutes**). If the price of gas falls, it becomes a better value way of heating a house compared with oil (if the price of oil remains constant). Economists refer to this as the **substitution effect**.
- Consumers are prepared to purchase more of a product only as its price falls. It is suggested that as more and more of a product is consumed, each extra unit of consumption yields less extra satisfaction. It is thus worth less to consumers and they will be prepared to pay less for it. Economists refer to this as the law of **diminishing marginal utility**.

It must be recalled that all this is true only so long as there is *ceteris paribus*. All other factors that could have an impact on demand must

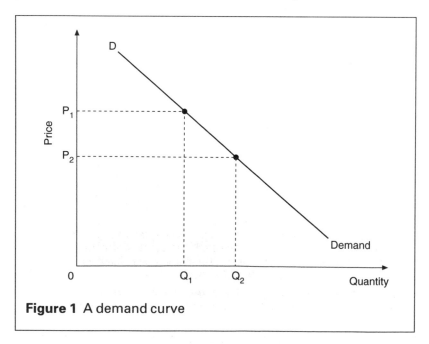

Figure 1 A demand curve

be held constant if solely the effect of price upon the quantity demanded is to be analysed.

The demand curve

The **demand curve** is a simple illustration of the relationship between the price of a product and the quantity demanded. Price is plotted on one axis and quantity demanded is plotted on the other axis. Given the law of demand, the shape of the demand curve will be as indicated in Figure 1.

The demand curve can be seen to slope downwards from left to right. At higher prices, less is demanded. At lower prices, more is demanded. If price were to fall (say from P_1 to P_2), the quantity demanded will rise (from Q_1 to Q_2).

Factors affecting demand

Price clearly has a major effect on the quantity of a product that is demanded. However, it is not the only factor that influences the

---

Air travel demand

The pace of Air Traffic Management (ATM) modernization depends in large part on how many aircraft the entire system must accommodate. The number of aircraft in the sky is dictated largely by consumer demand. Consumers value a variety of air travel aspects and attributes, many of which can be measured and quantified. Changes in ATM performance affect the quality of service and airline costs which together affect demand for airline services.

Price is only one aspect of an airline's product that consumers value; consumers also place value on service attributes as illustrated in the diagram.

Changes in different attributes evoke varying responses from consumers reflecting the value they place on each. This type of analysis will be useful in forecasting air carrier responses to ATM system changes and prioritizing improvements.

Source: mitre's corporation, 2000

Centre for Advanced Aviation System Development Working in the public interest, CAASD advances the safety, effectiveness and efficiency of aviation in the United States and around the world.

amount – other things, too, can have an important impact. This is clearly suggested in the article on air travel demand. Although the price of tickets matters, it is certainly suggested that other factors also have an impact on the demand for air travel.

The following factors can all have an important impact upon the demand for a product.

Consumers income

A change in the real income (that is, income allowing for the effects of inflation) of consumers is likely to have an impact upon the demand for a product. The usual possibility is that if a consumers income increases then the demand for a product will increase. The consumer can afford more of the product and therefore purchases more. As this is the usual situation, such products are referred to as **normal goods**.

It is possible in some cases that the relationship works in the opposite direction. With certain products, an increase in a consumers income can lead to a *lower* quantity of the product being demanded. This is because the products in question are purchased only because more desirable alternatives cannot be afforded. With an increase in income, the alternative can be purchased and the demand for the cheaper product thus falls. Given the nature of these products, they are termed **inferior goods**.

Luxury travel for less

Y ou do not have to pay the earth to get around in style. Here are some practical tips on how to travel first-class for less.

Try ticket agencies, as tickets that the reservations computer predicts will not be sold at full price are offloaded onto agencies and reduced in price. In some cases, you can find fares on well-known carriers at half the cost of published fares – with all the perks of a full-price ticket. Some of the biggest savings are on business-class tickets.

By paying an extra charge on some charter flights you can upgrade to premium class. Benefits may include wider seats with more leg-room. You may also receive free drinks, better food and service, and personal video screens.

Whether from economy to business, or from business to first – it's largely luck as to what seat upgrade you might get. However, there are certain things you can do to maximize your chances. If sections of the plane are overbooked, check-in staff may be looking for smartly dressed passengers who will be noted as 'suitable for upgrade' and approached by boarding staff.

The Daily Telegraph, 12 December 2001

It is not easy to generalize about what are inferior goods. It depends upon the starting income of the consumer concerned. One person's normal good could be another person's inferior good. Holidays are a product that might be deemed to be a normal product, but some holidays and related demands could be seen as more 'normal' than others. Some might even be deemed to be inferior. The article from *The Daily Telegraph* about luxury travel certainly suggests that certain travel products would be purchased if people could work out how to afford them. The implication might be that, as people's incomes rise, products such as economy seats on aeroplanes could be seen as inferior goods.

The price of other products

A change in the price of *other* products may affect the demand for the product in question. There are two ways in which this can happen.

Firstly, there may be **competitive demand**. This is a situation where the product faces competition from another product in terms of consumer demand. This happens when the products in question are *substitutes* – meaning that they are alternatives to each other. Examples of substitute products could include:

- travel by car or travel by train
- a pint of beer or a pint of lager
- an electric oven or a gas oven.

The relationship between the price of one substitute and the demand for the other can be easily predicted. If the price of beer goes up, then the demand for lager may rise. People may swap from buying beer to buying lager. If the price of travelling by train falls then fewer people may use their car. They swap from car use to the now cheaper alternative of the train. This can be described as a positive relationship. Price of the substitute product and demand for the product in question change in the same direction.

One important means through which competitive demand has been increased in recent years is through access to the Internet. This has opened up many new market possibilities to consumers. What this can be seen to be doing is to increase the number of substitute products that are available to consumers. There are many examples of this. The following article about the growth of Internet shopping indicates the growth of online shopping by the major supermarkets. This allows all consumers a greater choice of alternative products of many types.

Secondly, there may be **joint demand**. This happens when two products tend to be consumed together. Such products are described as **complements**.

Internet shopping keeps growing

SANDRA BARWICK

Waitrose's launch today of three further online shopping ventures confirms the explosion in supermarket Internet shopping.

Tesco, which on Monday added an online entertainment venture to its Internet shelves, expects to have a million customers by the end of the year. Sainsbury's is investing £30 million in e – business, including dedicated warehouses to serve Internet customers.

Waitrose, which already delivers wine through the Internet, is launching Organics Direct, offering boxed fruit and vegetables, Flowers Direct, which will also include champagne and chocolates and Waitrose Entertainment, delivering books, videos and CDs.

Tesco, which claims to be the world's largest online grocer with 250 000 registered customers and annual sales of £125 million, announced last week that 300 of its shops will soon offer its Tesco delivery service.

Marks & Spencer committed itself further to Internet trade, extending its experimental website *marks-and-spencer.com* from a small selection of gift ideas to 450 lines. It is also testing an Internet delivery service for its food products in Beaconsfield, Bucks.

The Daily Telegraph, 2 February 2000

There are many examples, including:

- fish and chips
- CDs and CD players
- personal computers and printers
- cars and petrol.

The relationship between the price of one complement and the demand for another is now different from the case with substitutes. If the price of cars falls then the demand for petrol will rise. If the price of computers rises then the demand for printers falls. There is thus an *inverse* relationship between the price of the complement and the demand for the product in question.

Tastes and fashions

Over a period of time, consumers **tastes** change. Fashions may come and they may go. Any such changes will cause a change in the demand for the product.

Caught up in the caffeine rush

It's the age-old problem. The evening is over and the young woman turns to her beau. 'Fancy coming in for a coffee?' she asks coyly. 'Coffee?' he asks incredulously. 'What do you mean? We've just passed five coffee bars on the way here. Why didn't you mention it before?'

The nation of tea drinkers is turning into one of caffeine addicts. Gone are the days when coffee drinkers were forced to sip brown sludge served by department stores' restaurants. Or to sit in cafes stuck in a fifties time warp, with ceilings stained by grease from the same era, served by waiters in black waistcoats and filthy white shirts.

Today the coffee bar, with its frightening array of drinks, cup sizes and prices is open on every major high street. Management consultants Allegra Strategies estimate that there are now 7100 coffee bars in Britain, of which just over 1300 are branded, with names such as Starbucks, Caffe Nero, Coffee Republic and Prêt á Manger, the upmarket sandwich chain.

This week Coffee Republic opened its 78th shop, while Costa, the country's largest coffee bar chain, announced plans to serve espressos on cruise ships. Laurie Morgan, marketing director at Costa, which sells 50 million cups a year, says: 'Good coffee is a treat that people can afford every day. It's a luxury. It's also leap years ahead of what people had been drinking. It's a lot like wine. For years Liebfraumilch was just fine but now people can taste the difference.' Supply, so it seems, creates its own demand. This is what has happened with coffee.

Jeffrey Young, consultant at Allegra, says: 'Two factors are driving this growth in demand. The biggest is because the coffee bars are there; but they are also seen as trendy places to socialize and conduct informal meetings. Women, for example, are attracted to coffee bars because they view them as less threatening than pubs to meet in, but anybody can go in by themselves to have a coffee and read a book or a newspaper.'

The Daily Telegraph, 14 April 2001

Many examples of such changes in tastes and fashions leading to a change in demand can be given. One clear example is suggested in the article from *The Daily Telegraph* about drinking coffee in coffee bars. A clear change in consumer tastes and fashions is seen as having a major impact upon the demand for this product.

Various factors can shape consumers tastes for products. However, the role of **advertising** is central. Producers are only prepared to spend large sums of money on advertising because they believe that it can have a significant effect upon the demand for their product. A successful advertising campaign will cause an increase in demand for the product and thus lead to greater profit potential. More of the product can now be sold at the same or even at a higher price.

Seasonal variations

There are many examples of consumer demand that can be described as **seasonal**. The demand for the product varies depending upon the time of the year. Typical examples of this are:

- holidays abroad or at home
- different types of clothing
- sports equipment for different sports
- toys (especially in the lead-up to Christmas)
- different types of food.

Expectations about future price movements

An interesting factor affecting current demand may be future **expectations** about price. If there is an anticipation that price will change in the future, then that could have an impact upon demand *today*. The simple rule can be described as follows:

- If the price of the product is expected to rise, then present demand will increase. Consumers will wish to purchase before the price rises.
- If the price of the product is expected to fall, then present demand will fall. Consumers will not wish to purchase the product until the price has fallen.

Such possibilities can exist in the market for many products. However, they are particularly evident in financial markets. The demand for the shares of a company on the stock exchange is fundamentally determined by the views of investors about what is likely to happen to price in the future. In such markets, this can lead to **self-fulfilling prophecies**. The anticipated increase in price can lead to higher demand. This in turn can cause price to rise. This is discussed further in Chapter Five on price determination.

Changes in demand and the demand curve

Any change in demand can be illustrated through a demand curve. However, there is an important difference between the effects of a change in the price of a product and all other factors that may cause demand to change.

A change in demand due to a change in price

Any change in demand due to a change in the price of the product is shown by a movement along the demand curve. The demand curve itself does not move. This is indicated in Figure 2.

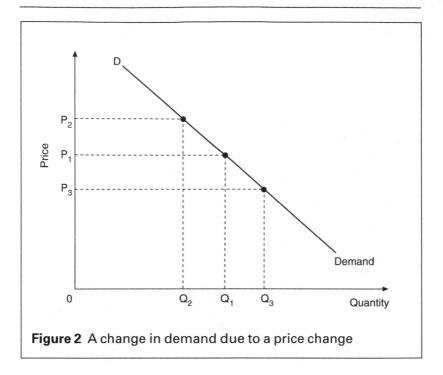

Figure 2 A change in demand due to a price change

The starting price is indicated by price P_1.

- An increase in price to P_2 causes demand to fall to quantity Q_2. This is described as a **contraction of demand**.
- A reduction in price to P_3 causes demand to increase to quantity Q_3. This is referred to as an **extension of demand**.

A change in demand due to a change in a non-price factor

Any other reason, apart from the change in price of the product, that may cause demand to change is illustrated in a different way on the demand diagram. All other factors, such as a change in income or the price of an alternative product, cause the demand schedule (curve) to shift. Different amounts are now demanded at the same price. This is illustrated in Figure 3. The original demand curve is D_1.

- An **increase in demand** is illustrated by a rightward movement in the demand schedule (to D_2). More is demanded at the same price (P_1).
- A **decrease in demand** is illustrated by a leftward movement in the demand schedule (to D_3). Less is demanded at the same price (P_1).

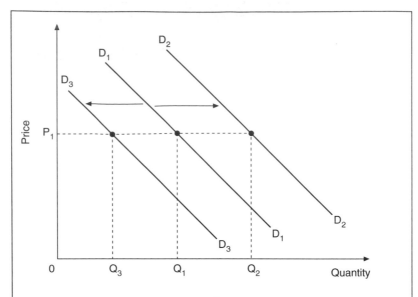

Figure 3 A change in demand due to a change in a non-price factor

Individual and market demand curves

Every individual person has a demand curve for any product for which he or she might have a potential interest in purchasing. Different quantities of a product would be bought by an individual at different prices. For larger products, it may be a matter of a particular price at which the individual is prepared to purchase one product.

The demand curve for a whole market for a product is simply the addition of all the relevant individual demand schedules. If there are 1000 possible consumers in a market, then the summation of all 1000 individual demand curves will give the total **market demand curve**. All these schedules are added horizontally to give the total market schedule as indicated in Figure 4.

Consumer surplus

When a product is sold in a market, it is usually sold at just one price. Different consumers all have to purchase the same product at the same price. This is despite the fact that different consumers may have been prepared to pay different prices for the same product. In this sense, some consumers may be seen to get a 'good deal'. They pay less for the

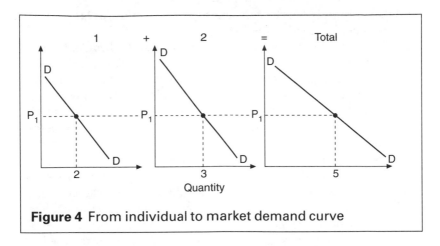

Figure 4 From individual to market demand curve

product than they would have been prepared to pay for it. The value of this 'good deal' is called **consumer surplus.**

Consumer surplus is the difference between the price that a consumer is prepared to pay for a product and the actual selling price of the product. If a customer is willing to pay £15 for a particular CD but is able to purchase that CD at the current selling price of £10, then the

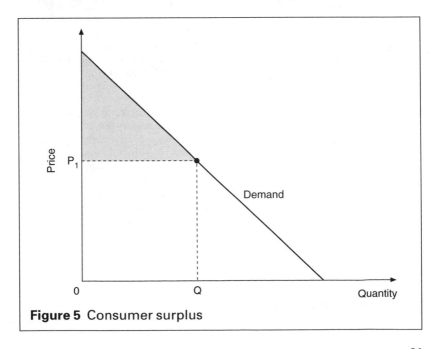

Figure 5 Consumer surplus

consumer surplus is £5.The consumer gains a surplus (or 'good deal') worth £5 when purchasing the CD.

Consumer surplus can be illustrated on a demand schedule. Figure 5 indicates that if the selling price of the product is P_1 then there is a consumer surplus equal to the value of the shaded area in this market. Consumer Q was prepared to pay just P_1 for this product. However, all previous consumers were prepared to pay more. As they all had to pay only P_1, there is consumer surplus gained by all consumers before consumer Q. The shaded area shows the value of the consumer surpluses of all consumers in this market added together.

Sometimes, entrepreneurs attempt to charge different prices to different customers in order to try to get hold of some of this consumer surplus. A good example of this is the operation of ticket touts. Such operators buy tickets at the official price knowing that there are people who are willing to pay more than this for the tickets. They then sell the tickets on to those consumers at a higher price (thus making a profit). This can be seen, for example, in major sporting fixtures that are very popular. *The Observer* article about England's rugby fixture against Italy indicates this practice.

March arrives a month early

VIC MARKS

A crowd of 75 000 was crammed into Twickenham to witness what everyone – including the English team at the start – assumed was a foregone conclusion: an easy England victory over Italy. This may not be a unique occurrence but it is a strange one.

So it takes some head-scratching to explain why so many ticket touts were on parade outside the ground yesterday. The RFU must be laughing all the way to the bank. 75 000 were happy to pay for tickets. Many of them were happy to pay well in excess of the official selling price charged by the RFU.

But why was demand so great for tickets? Has a Twickenham ticket become an essential status symbol, with the ability to acquire one suggesting a man – or woman – of influence? Maybe the brand of rugby that England have been playing is so irresistible that a trip to south-west London was justified just to see Woodward's wizards embark on a glorified practice session. Whatever it was, people were prepared to pay a lot of money for it.

Adapted from *The Observer*, 18 February 2001

```
                        KEY WORDS

Wants                          Competitive demand
Demand                         Joint demand
Notional demand                Complements
Effective demand               Tastes
Ceteris paribus                Advertising
Law of demand                  Seasonal
Rational (consumers)           Expectations
Utility                        Self-fulfilling prophecies
Income effect                  Expectations
Substitutes                    Contraction of demand
Substitution effect            Extension of demand
Diminishing marginal utility   Increase of demand
Demand curve                   Decrease in demand
Normal goods                   Market demand curve
Inferior goods                 Consumer surplus
```

Further reading

Bamford, C. (ed.), Unit 1 in *Economics for AS*, Cambridge University Press, 2000.

Grant, S., Chapter 8 in *Stanlake's Introductory Economics*, 7th edn, Longman, 2000.

Grant, S. and Vidler, C., Part 1, Unit 5 in *Economics in Context*, Heinemann Educational, 2000.

Parkin, M., Powell, M. and Matthews, K., Chapter 4 in *Economics*, 4th edn, Pearson Educational, 2000.

Useful websites

- Air travel: www.lastminute.com
- Coffee shops: www.eats.co.uk/coffeeshops

Essay topics

1. It has been claimed by the government that Britain will need an extra 4.5 million homes in the next 25 years. Examine the possible reasons for this anticipated extra demand for homes. [20 marks] [Edexcel, June 1999]

2. (a) Explain why demand curves slope down from the left to the right. [8 marks]
   (b) Analyse the effect of an increase in consumers' income on the demand for

    (i)   holidays in Blackpool

    (ii) holidays in the Bahamas.   [12 marks]

Data response question

This question refers to an article 'Air Travel demand' on page 13.

1. (a) Define the term 'demand'.   [2 marks]

    (b) Explain the relationship between the price of a product and the quantity of that product that is demanded.   [3 marks]

2. Using demand diagrams illustrate the effects of the following on the demand for air travel

    (a) an increase in the price of airline tickets   [5 marks]

    (b) a perceived increase in the safety of air travel   [5 marks]

3. Discuss how airline companies can use the information in the article in order to develop their product and set their prices.   [10 marks]

Chapter Three

Elasticities of demand

'Demand for air travel is highly elastic'

The Economist, 30 June 2001

Our analysis in the last chapter explained that many factors can affect the demand for a particular good or service. Consider air travel, for example. In that highly competitive market, price is likely to be the most important factor affecting demand. It is particularly important in determining the number of seats sold by an airline on any given route. There are of course other factors to be considered, such as the income of air travellers, the availability of substitutes such as rail, coach or car travel, and whether or not someone really does like flying. The ticket price paid, though, is likely for most travellers to determine whether they actually make a particular journey.

The basic principles of demand, as stated in *Chapter Two*, are:

- If the price of a good increases, demand will fall.
- Put another way, more of a good will be demanded at a lower price.

What these principles do *not* tell us is *by how much* the quantity that is demanded falls or increases in response to a change in price. This is the concept of the **price elasticity of demand**.

The idea of elasticity is wider than this and can be applied to explain how demand responds to a change in any of its determinants. Two further important concepts are:

- **income elasticity of demand** – how demand responds to a change in consumers income
- **cross elasticity of demand** – how demand responds to a change in the price of goods that are substitutes or complements.

Elasticity therefore is a measure of how much buyers respond to changes in market conditions. The reference in *The Economist* to the market for air travel is a general statement which seems to indicate that the market is very responsive to any changes in market conditions.

Price elasticity of demand

Price elasticity of demand is a measure of how much the quantity demanded for a good or service responds to a change in its price. More precisely, it is measured as follows:

Price elasticity of demand

$$= \frac{\text{percentage change in quantity demanded}}{\text{percentage change in price}}$$

The outcome therefore is a number, which is usually negative, reflecting the fact that most demand curves slope downwards.

Returning to the example of air travel, suppose the price of an air ticket between Manchester and London increases from £200 to £220. Suppose also that this increase causes demand to fall from 10 000 trips per month to 8 000 trips per month. Therefore:

Percentage change in quantity demanded

$$= \frac{\text{change in quantity demanded}}{\text{original quantity}} \times 100 \text{ per cent}$$

$$= \frac{-2000}{10\,000} \times 100 = -20 \text{ per cent}$$

and

Percentage change in price

$$= \frac{\text{change in price}}{\text{original price}} \times 100 \text{ per cent}$$

$$= \frac{20}{200} \times 100 = 10 \text{ per cent.}$$

Putting this data into the above formula, we obtain:

$$\text{Price elasticity of demand} = \frac{-20 \text{ per cent}}{10 \text{ per cent}} = -2.$$

In this example, therefore, the price elasticity of demand figure indicates that the change in quantity demanded is proportionately twice as large as the change in price.

It is common practice to ignore the negative sign, reporting all price elasticities as 'absolute' values. As indicated, for virtually all goods and services, the demand curve is downward-sloping, so illustrating an inverse relationship between price and quantity demanded. With this in mind, it follows that the larger the value of price elasticity of demand, the greater will be the responsiveness of the quantity demanded to a change in price.

Not all goods or services that we buy are responsive to price changes. This is particularly true of goods that are often regarded as **necessities**, such as water, bread and petrol. In each case, if prices were to rise by say twenty per cent, there would be only a small fall in the quantities that are demanded. It is difficult to cut back on the amount of water we need; bread is an important part of our staple diet; and for motorists and haulage companies, petrol is essential for everyday personal and business needs. So, in these cases, it is likely that the quantity demanded would fall a little, but nowhere approaching the twenty per cent rise in price. Such goods are therefore not very responsive to a change in price.

Determinants of price elasticity of demand

As identified above, the extent to which demand for goods and services is price responsive varies. So, what determines this? The answer largely relates back to the determinants of demand which were analysed in the last chapter. It is these factors – economic, social and psychological – that determine consumer preferences, and hence the price elasticity of demand for a good or service. Five main determinants can be recognized.

Is the good or service a necessity or a luxury item?

The earlier examples have shown that the demand for necessary goods is not very responsive to price changes. The demand for basic foodstuffs and everyday items essential for daily living is unlikely to be affected by a small price change. Bus travel, for those who do not own a car, is unlikely to be much affected by a fare increase.

In contrast, the demand for luxury goods, that is non-essential products, is much more likely to be price sensitive. So, for holidays, most types of clothing, eating out and high-class food items, a change in price is likely to produce a much greater change in the quantities that are demanded. It is not easy to generalize here as what is considered a necessity for some may well be a luxury item for higher income earners. A Mediterranean cruise could be thought essential by a stressed-out City banker, yet a luxury good for someone on a much lower income.

The availability and closeness of substitutes

Most consumer goods have substitutes (see *Chapter Two*). Those that have close substitutes tend to have a more responsive demand to price changes than goods which do not have close substitutes.

A much-quoted example is that of Coca Cola and Pepsi Cola, two very similar branded products. Their closeness means that their demand is highly sensitive to changes in their prices. So, if the price of Coca Cola falls, then the demand for Pepsi Cola is likely to fall, and vice versa. The extent of this change in demand is likely to be more than the fall in price unless there is substantial brand loyalty in the market.

Britain takes to the air

The air of gloom surrounding much of European business made Ryanair's results, announced on June 25th, particularly impressive. The low-cost airline reported a 37 per cent year-on-year increase in pre-tax profits. ...

Air travel in and around Britain has grown by nearly 40 per cent in the past five years, but the really spectacular growth has come from the low-fare airlines, which have carried around 20m passengers in the past year. By spotting and satisfying the untapped demand for travel from and between the regions, they have fuelled the growth of Britain's smaller airports and undermined Heathrow's dominance.

EasyJet, the first of the low-cost carriers, was set up in 1995 at Luton. Eastwards around the M25 at Stansted are Ryanair, Go, the low-cost offshoot

Cheaper and faster

	Time (hrs)
Ryanair	1:10
EasyJet	1:15
Virgin trains	5:20
GNER	1:20
Go	5:18
British Airways	1:10

0   50   100   150   200

Price of tickets booked on 27 June for travel on 29 June from London to Glasgow (£)

to British Airways (BA) sold to a management buy-out earlier this year, and Buzz, the British arm of KLM, which uses the airline partly to feed its international hub at Amsterdam. While Heathrow has seen the number of passengers rise by about 19 per cent over that period, traffic at Luton and Stansted has more than trebled (see the chart). Traffic at Liverpool's airport nearly quadrupled.

Demand for air travel is highly elastic. Bring down the price and sales rise sharply. The low-fare carriers are often cheaper not just than the mainstream operators but also than the railways. While low-fare airlines keep their costs to a minimum, the railways are burdened by the need to maintain and improve their crumbling network. ...

Low-cost airlines fill their planes differently from mainstream carriers. BA, British Midland, Air France and Lufthansa aim to make their money out of business travellers who pay to enjoy meals and drinks in the air and on the ground in exclusive lounges. The economy seats are sold off, discounted as need be, some in advance and some at the last minute. Cheap seats are made available through downmarket travel agencies.

The low-cost carriers see their aircraft as a series of buckets. The first set of buckets are the lowest-priced seats, with the eye-catching prices. Once these are all sold, demand flows into the next, slightly more expensive, buckets of seats. As the flight's departure approaches, seats get progressively more expensive. On a typical low-cost flight there could be up to ten different price buckets. But even the most expensive tickets tend to be cheaper than for the mainstream airlines.

Adapted from *The Economist*, 30 June 2001

Where there are no close substitutes, for example eggs and flour, demand is most unlikely to be price sensitive.

The market for air travel again provides some interesting examples (see the accompanying box from *The Economist*). This market is becoming more price sensitive, with low-cost carriers increasingly competing with established national scheduled airlines. For travel in the UK, in turn, there is extensive price competition between air and rail, as the article indicates.

The product definition and its market

It is important to distinguish between the substitutability of products in the *same* group and substitutability of goods from other product groupings. For example, different types of coffee are a group of products in their own right; they are also part of a larger group of non-alcoholic drink products and part of an even bigger category of products that we could label simply 'drinks'. A very specific named product such as Nescafé Gold Blend instant coffee will probably have a demand which is quite responsive to a price change. As we aggregate products into broader groupings, their demand is likely to be less responsive to a price change.

The relative expense of a good or service

This issue has already been raised in the context of necessity and luxury items. Any change in the price of a good will affect the purchasing power or real income of a consumer of that product. The larger the proportion of income the price of that product represents, the more likely that demand will be responsive to a change in price. For example, a ten per cent increase in the price of a holiday is likely to have a bigger impact on a consumer than a ten per cent increase in commuter rail fares.

The time factor

In the short term, consumers find it hard to change their spending patterns. Over a longer period of time, though, demand may well become more sensitive to changes in price, as consumers adjust and adapt their spending plans.

Comment

Of the five determinants that have been identified above, for most goods and services the key influence on price elasticity of demand is the availability or otherwise of close substitutes in the same or lower price range. All of the other influences tend to be connected to this.

We can take car models as an example. Purely as a *means of transport*, a Nissan Micra may be a substitute for an Audi TT. Someone buying the latter is most unlikely to even consider buying the former, whereas another small economy car could well be considered depending on the relative prices. The price elasticity of demand for the Micra will therefore be more elastic than for an Audi TT.

Furthermore, although air and rail are undoubtedly vastly different modes of transport, they too can be considered as close substitutes for the longer journeys people have to make in the UK. Their respective demand is very responsive to changes in the fares that are charged.

What do the numbers mean?

The estimates that are calculated for price elasticity of demand are very important to economists, for three reasons:

- They indicate whether the demand for a good or service is responsive to a change in its price.
- They may provide the basis on which demand curves can be classified, given the same scaling on the axes. The value of the price elasticity of demand determines whether the demand curve is steep or flat.
- They can be used to forecast the effects of a price change on the demand for a good or service. In particular, they can be used to see whether revenue from sales of that product have increased or not.

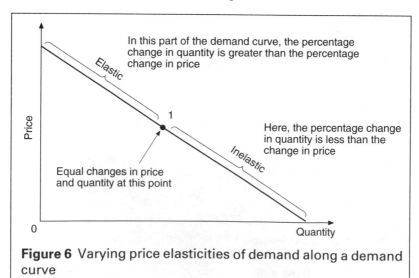

Figure 6 Varying price elasticities of demand along a demand curve

Two important benchmarks are:

- Where the price elasticity of demand is greater than 1, then demand is **elastic**. This means that the quantity demanded changes more than the change in price.
- Where the price elasticity of demand is less than 1, then demand is **inelastic**. This means that the quantity demanded changes less than the change in price.

As a useful rule of thumb, the flatter the demand curve that passes through a given point, the greater is the price elasticity of demand. Alternatively, the steeper the demand curve at a given point, then the smaller is the price elasticity of demand.

Along any straight-line demand curve, the price elasticity of demand will vary from zero to infinity. There is a section that is price elastic and one which is price inelastic, as shown in Figure 6. This characteristic is very important from a business standpoint, as we shall see later.

Figure 7 shows how, for a given fall in price of a good, the price elasticity of demand varies depending upon the shape of the demand curve. The figure shows the perfectly elastic and inelastic cases, (a) and (e), and three less extreme cases, (b), (c) and (d). When an elasticity estimate may be known, the likely shape of the demand curve can be projected from the number that has been provided.

From a business standpoint, knowing the price elasticity of demand is very important when a firm is planning its pricing policy or taking other important strategic decisions – such as how to increase market share. It is also used in pricing and marketing decisions taken by businesses such as passenger train operators, or hotels that have a 'perishable' product. The basis for such decisions is the relationship between price elasticity of demand and a firm's revenue.

The **total revenue** or sales of a firm in any market is simply calculated by P × Q, the price of the good or service multiplied by the quantity that is sold. The total revenue changes as one moves along the demand curve. The extent of the change depends upon the price elasticity of demand at that point on the demand curve (see Figure 8).

The total revenue is shown on Figure 8 by the area under the demand curves. These curves are both taken from Figure 7 and show what happens to total revenue when the price of the good falls from £5 to £4. More generally, we can state the following:

- With an inelastic demand curve, a decrease in price leads to a proportionately smaller increase in quantity. Total revenue

31

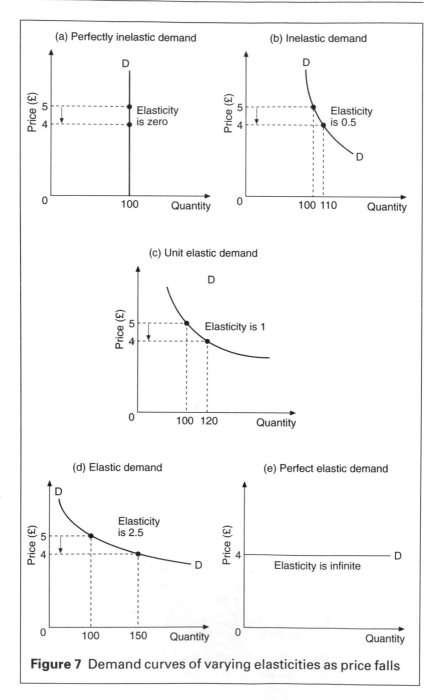

Figure 7 Demand curves of varying elasticities as price falls

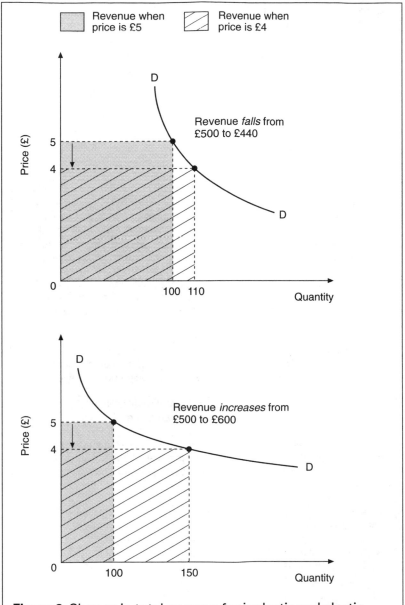

Figure 8 Change in total revenue for inelastic and elastic demand situations

therefore falls. An increase in price will lead to a proportionately smaller decrease in quantity. Total revenue will increase.

- With an elastic demand curve, a decrease in price leads to a proportionately greater increase in quantity. Total revenue therefore increases. An increase in price will lead to a proportionately greater decrease in quantity. Total revenue will decrease.

What fare?

Price elasticity of demand is the key

Buying a rail ticket from one of the UK's train operating companies is by no means straightforward. It can be a difficult and sometimes expensive experience, especially if you are not aware of the full range of tickets (and fares) available. Train operators such as GNER, Virgin Trains and Midland Main Line have been very clever in the way they have sought to segment their market for long distance travel, to London especially. They aim to maximize their revenue and seat occupancies by exploiting the fact that price is an important factor in the decision to travel, whilst for some groups of traveller their decision to travel is price inelastic. In general:

Price inelastic   – Business travellers, regular commuters
                  – Travellers arriving at their destination before 10.00 a.m.
                  – 'Walk on travellers' who buy a ticket on the day of travel
Price elastic   – Leisure travellers
                  – Travellers for whom time of arrival is flexible
                  – Travellers able to book in advance

The more flexible travellers can be in their plans, then the cheaper the fare is likely to be. For example, the following were typical return fares on Virgin Trains services between Manchester and London Euston in late 2001:

£236	£164	£52.30	£20
1st class Open	Standard Open	Saver	14-day advance
No restrictions: travel at any time, buy at any time		Cannot be used for peak-time travel, but buy at any time	Must be purchased in advance on nominated trains (off-peak travel in the main, no flexibility)

Price inelastic   ←――――――――――――――――→   Price elastic

It should now be clear that if a firm decides to cut prices to increase the number of sales, it does not necessarily follow that its sales revenue will increase. If the firm has a product for which demand is inelastic, there is no point whatsoever in cutting prices – this will only reduce the firms total revenue. If it is trying to gain market share from a rival, then its best strategy is some form of **non-price competition**. It could, for example, have a special promotion (for example 'Buy one, get one free') or it could pursue an extensive advertising campaign, both of which would raise the standing of their product in the preferences of potential consumers.

When a firms demand is price elastic, notably where there are close substitutes, then even a modest reduction in price could increase sales quite significantly by getting existing customers to buy more and by attracting customers from brand rivals. In the highly competitive grocery market, this strategy has been used from time to time by companies such as Heinz, Nestlé and Kelloggs, each of which have brand leader products in their own markets. The business logic behind this strategy has been one of winning back customers from rival supermarket own-brand products in an attempt to maintain overall market share. High-powered advertising campaigns usually operate alongside price cuts as a means of retaining product superiority in the preferences of consumers.

Finally, price elasticity of demand estimates are used by economists when making forecasts. The Department of Transport, for example, uses a price elasticity of demand for air travel of -1.0 in its air traffic forecasts for the UK. This figure reflects a lower elasticity for business markets and a higher elasticity for leisure markets. These forecasts are made for five-year intervals over the period to 2020. The price of air travel, taking into account projected fuel prices and landing charges, is taken as the most important variable in determining future traffic growth.

How is price elasticity of demand estimated?

The calculation of price elasticity of demand is very simple ... provided you have the data! This can pose a particular problem for a business because the nature of the price elasticity concept is that it requires accurate information to be available for two different points in time. In other words, it is necessary to have two sets of price and quantity information to be able to calculate a price elasticity estimate. It should also be stressed that for the elasticity estimate to be credible, the information must be accurate and reliable.

In business, the data can be collected in two main ways.

- *Past records*. Most companies will have records of the sales of their products at different prices over a particular time period. In principle this could be used to calculate the price elasticity of demand for that product, provided it is understood that the estimate is based on all other factors affecting demand remaining unchanged. The further back in time the researcher has to go, the less likely that this assumption will apply.
- *Consumer surveys*. Here, a representative group of consumers are asked how much of a particular product they might buy at various prices. Alternatively, consumers who have bought a product at a known price could be asked how much more or how much less they might have bought at a lower or higher price. The accuracy of this method is somewhat suspect since it relies on consumers being asked hypothetical questions on possible future purchases.

So, it should be remembered that price elasticity figures are usually estimates, having been compiled from information which may itself be subject to some degree of statistical variability. It is therefore essential for businesses using price elasticity information to do their utmost to ensure that important business decisions are being taken based on robust and reasonably accurate information.

Income elasticity of demand

So far our discussion of elasticity has been based on price elasticity of demand. As we saw in *Chapter Two*, there are factors other than price that can affect the demand for a good. Of these, income is particularly important – whether someone can afford to buy a particular good determines whether their demand is effective rather than notional.

Income elasticity of demand is a measure of how responsive demand for a product or service is in relation to a change in consumers income. It is calculated as follows:

Income elasticity of demand

$$= \frac{\text{percentage change in quantity demanded}}{\text{percentage change in income}}$$

The outcome of this calculation is a number, and whether this is positive or negative is of particular significance. Where the value for income elasticity of demand is positive, then as income increases, so too does demand. In contrast, a negative value indicates that the quantity demanded falls as income increases.

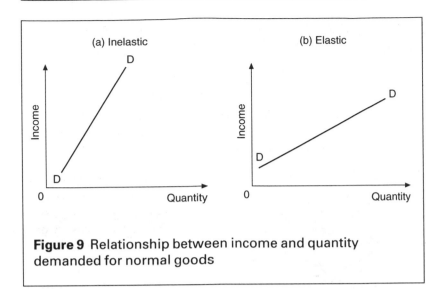

Figure 9 Relationship between income and quantity demanded for normal goods

Let us look at a new example, but again involving air travel. Suppose that, over a year, household income increases by ten per cent and the demand for air travel increases by thirty per cent. Inserting this information into the above formula, we can see that the income elasticity of demand is +3.

The positive sign indicates that air travel is a **normal good**. Most goods and services fall into this category – higher incomes raise the quantity that is demanded. This situation is shown in Figure 9. The two income/consumption lines have positive gradients – the one on the right is much more sensitive to a change in income than the one on the left. Where the income elasticity of demand is above 1, then these goods are said to be *income elastic*. For example, many consumer goods are like this, including products such as mobile phones, organic food, overseas holidays and eating out. Other goods may still be normal goods yet their demand is *income inelastic* – an increase in income will increase demand but at a rate of increase below the increase in income. The income elasticity estimate in this case would be between 0 and 1.

Income elasticity is best seen empirically over a reasonable time period. Figure 10, taken from the General Household Expenditure Survey, provides some insight into the likely income elasticities of demand for certain consumer durable goods.

Those products with the steepest time trend are likely to have an income elastic demand. This is especially true where a new product is launched in the market, for example a CD player in 1990 or a video

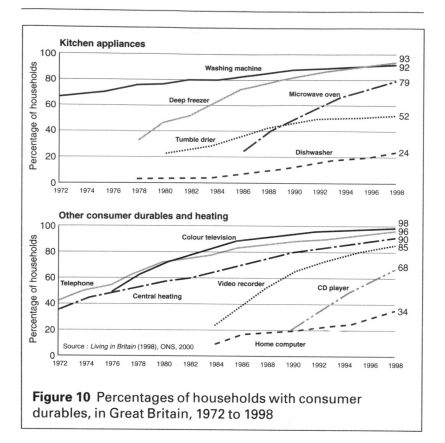

Figure 10 Percentages of households with consumer durables, in Great Britain, 1972 to 1998

recorder in 1984. Excluding products where consumption is at saturation levels, it is interesting to compare the time trend for CD players and video recorders with that for dishwashers and home computers. For the latter pair, the increase in consumption has been steady but slight for much of the period – in the case of home computers, demand appears to have accelerated towards the end of the period shown in Figure 10.

Dishwashers and home computers are much more likely to be found in professional households rather than in unskilled manual households. It should though be stressed that Figure 10 is a crude market generalization – individual choice and preference will clearly determine consumption for many households.

Recent research at Leeds University has shown that the income elasticity of demand for rail travel in Great Britain is between +1.5 and +2.5. There is some geographical variation between different route corridors, with the largest increases in demand being recorded in conurbations outside London. The research has also shown that, over time, the income elasticity of demand for rail travel has increased.

A small number of goods and services are known as **inferior goods**. As their name suggests, as incomes rise, the demand for inferior goods falls. In such cases the income elasticity of demand will be negative. The gradient of the income consumption line will also be negative (see Figure 11). Returning to our transport examples, coach travel is likely to be an inferior good for many families. When given alternatives, if they can afford it, many will use rail or air travel in preference to the coach for long-distance travel. So, if over a year, household income increases by ten per cent and the demand for coach travel falls by thirty per cent, the income elasticity of demand is −3.

It is really quite difficult to obtain data on inferior goods. As incomes rise then it is likely that families will spend less on second-hand goods, public transport and cheap food items and substitute better quality products in their place. The Family Expenditure Survey provides some very limited evidence on how expenditure patterns change as incomes increase. Most notably, expenditure on food and non-alcoholic drink decreases as a percentage of household income as incomes rise. Expenditure on fuel and light also falls. These products in general are

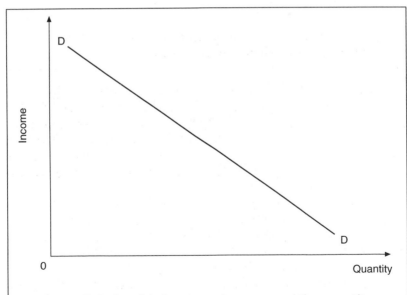

Figure 11 Relationship between income and the quantity demanded of an inferior good

not really inferior goods; the relative decline in consumption is more indicative of **Engel's law** – that as people become better off, a smaller proportion of their income is expended on essential goods and services.

Cross elasticity of demand

A third elasticity measure used in economics is that of cross elasticity of demand. This estimate is derived from the fact that, as shown in *Chapter Two*, the price of complements and substitutes can affect the demand for a particular good or service. Let us look at a few examples.

In recent years the price of petrol and diesel has increased in real terms (although it fell quite dramatically in 2001). As a consequence of the price rise it is more economical for motorists to run cars with small engines such as the Nissan Micra and the Toyota Yaris than it is to run large-engined cars. So, as petrol is a complementary good to a car, the increase in petrol prices has prompted a switch to smaller, cheaper vehicles. The demand for other forms of transport can also be linked to changes in fuel prices.

Cross elasticity of demand is a measure of how much the quantity demanded for one good or service responds to a change in the price of *another* good or service. It is calculated as follows:

Cross elasticity of demand

$$= \frac{\text{percentage change in demand for good X}}{\text{percentage change in price of good Y}}$$

So, suppose over a year, say, the price of petrol increases by fifteen per cent, and in turn the demand for large-engined vehicles falls by five per cent. The estimate of cross elasticity of demand will be −5%/+15% = −0.33. The negative sign here indicates that the two goods are *complements*.

The estimate is inelastic, indicating that the strength of the relationship is relatively weak. Presumably owners of high-powered cars are not over-bothered about the rise in petrol prices. The relationship behind this is shown in Figure 12.

The reverse is true where the goods are *substitutes*. Again, taking cars as our example, government policy is to encourage more motorists to use smaller cars by reducing the annual vehicle excise duty which is paid on them relative to larger engined vehicles. This results in a slight fall in the operating costs of such vehicles. In theory, it could be expected to reduce the demand for cars with large engines. Suppose, over a year, the operating costs of small vehicles falls by two per cent

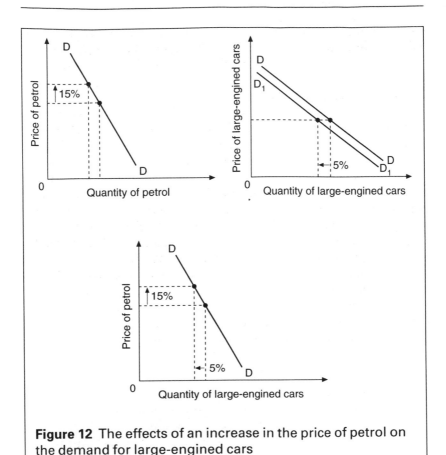

Figure 12 The effects of an increase in the price of petrol on the demand for large-engined cars

and the demand for large vehicles falls by three per cent. The value of the cross elasticity of demand for large cars with respect to the cost of running a small car will be –3%/–2% = +1.5. The positive sign here indicates that the goods are substitutes and the estimate is elastic, showing that motorists are in fact taking note of what the government is expecting them to do. The relationship is shown in Figure 13.

Estimates of cross elasticity of demand tell us about the relationship between two goods. The *sign* (positive in the case of substitutes, negative for complements) is the key to this, whereas the *size* of the estimate tells us about the strength or weakness of the relationship. The higher the number, then the stronger is the relationship between the two goods.

Obtaining data on cross elasticities of demand is not easy. In general,

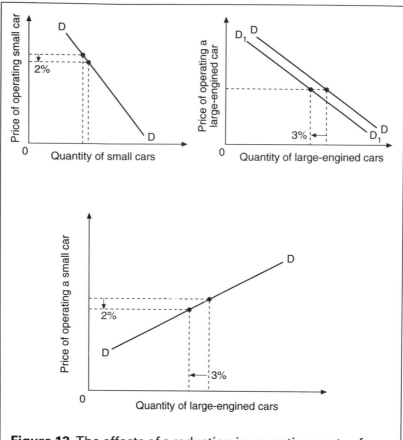

Figure 13 The effects of a reduction in operating costs of a small car on the demand for large-engined cars

specific investigations have to be made in order to estimate the relationships involved over a very specific time period. A knowledge of cross elasticity of demand is, though, useful in certain business situations. In retailing, for example, the relationship between two brands of instant coffee or between an own-label and a branded product can help a retailer to decide on a pricing strategy. Another application could be in the holiday market where it is useful for tour operators to know how a change in price could affect the demand for holidays at competing destinations.

Conclusion

In this chapter we have shown that the concept of elasticity of demand is very important to businesses in understanding how their markets work and how they should respond to changes in market conditions. Elasticity is a very pertinent example of how economic theory can be appropriately applied to particular business situations. The quotation from *The Economist* at the head of this chapter is typical of the relevance of this important concept of market economics.

KEY WORDS

Price elasticity of demand	Total revenue
Income elasticity of demand	Non-price competition
Cross elasticity of demand	Normal good
Necessities	Inferior goods
Elastic	Engel's law
Inelastic	

Further reading

Anderton, A., Unit 9 in *Economics*, 3rd edn, Causeway Press, 2000.

Bamford, C. (ed.), Unit 1, section 2 in *Economics for AS*, Cambridge University Press, 2000.

Grant, S., Chapter 9 in *Stanlake's Introductory Economics*, 7th edn, Longman, 2000.

Grant, S., and Vidler, C., Part 1, Unit 6 in *Economics in Context*, Heinemann Educational, 2000.

Useful website

Department of Transport: www.dt.gov.uk

Essay topics

1. Market research for a large tour operator has estimated that the price elasticity of demand for holidays booked one year ahead of departure is −1.8 and that for holidays booked within one month of departure is −0.2. As a consequence, the company decided to increase the prices for its 'late booked' holidays by £20 per person.
   (a) Explain what these price elasticity of demand estimates mean and why they might differ. [10 marks]
   (b) Discuss the relevance of the above information to the tour operator's overall pricing policy. [15 marks]

[OCR, March 2000]

2. A national cinema chain has the following information:
   (i)   The income elasticity of demand for visits to the cinema is +2.5.
   (ii) The price elasticity of demand for visits to the cinema is –2.2.
   (iii) The cross elasticity of demand for visits to the cinema with respect to the rental payment of pre-recorded video films is +3.8.
   (iv) The cross elasticity of demand for visits to the cinema with respect to the price of popcorn sold in the cinema is –1.0.

   Examine the significance of each of these figures for the cinema company. [60 marks]
   [Edexcel, June 1998]

Data response question

This task is based on a question set by OCR in January 2001.
Read the following article and study the two tables. Then answer the questions that follow.

Steady Haul Logistics

Steady Haul Logistics is a small road transport and warehousing company based in the West Midlands. It transports goods and operates a separate storage business in its warehouses. It is just one of many such companies in this part of England. The company's owner, Eddie Shifter, has seen the business grow in recent years to its current size of twenty goods vehicles and five warehouses.

The company is operating in a fiercely competitive market, where price is the main reason why customers choose one transport firm rather than another. Eddie's own research for his business, summarized in Table A, shows this very clearly. He is, however, increasingly concerned about rising fuel prices, which account for 35 per cent of his total costs.

Eddie and his company are currently facing a major dilemma – should they continue to offer both transport and warehouse services at the present level or would it be better to use existing resources differently by selling off some vehicles and increasing the warehouse capacity available to its customers?

Table A Weekly demand schedule for road transport services

Price per km (£)	Quantity demanded (kms)
14	500
12	1000
10	3000
8	6000
6	9000
4	12000
2	14000

1. (a) Use the information in Table A to draw the demand curve for road transport services. [3 marks]
   (b) Describe briefly what this curve indicates. [2 marks]
   (c) Using a diagram, explain how a fall in the price of *rail* freight might affect the demand for road transport services. [5 marks]

2. (a) Define price elasticity of demand. [2 marks]
   (b) Use the information in Table A to calculate the price elasticity of demand for transport services as the price decreases from £8 to £6. [2 marks]
   (c) Describe how Eddie might have estimated the data shown in Table A. [4 marks]
   (d) Explain what use the business can make of price elasticity of demand estimates such as that calculated above. [6 marks]

Chapter Four

Supply

'It is not from the benevolence of the butcher, the brewer, or the baker that we expect our dinner, but from their regard to their own self interest.'
Adam Smith, *The Wealth of Nations*.

If demand stems from the 'infinite wants' side of the economic problem, then supply is the other side of the equation. It considers what can be produced with the scarce resources that are available to meet the infinite wants of consumers.

Defining supply

The supply of a product depends upon the actions of producers. It is **producers** who turn scarce resources into consumer goods and services in order to meet the demands of consumers. Why do they do this?

In economics, the standard assumption is that they do this in order to make profits. The motivation for producers, in their fundamental role in helping to tackle the economic problem, is to maximize profits. It is not simply to be helpful to others that products are made, but it is to make profits. This is important in understanding the concept of supply in economics.

With this in mind, it is possible to define 'supply'.

> Supply represents the amounts of a product that producers are willing and able to supply at different market prices over a given time period.

The decision will be dictated by the profit possibilities that there are perceived to be at these different prices.

The relationship between supply and price

As with demand, which we looked at in *Chapter Two*, a fundamental question with regard to supply is how it can be expected to change as price changes. How will producers react to changes in the market price of the product? If price rises, will suppliers seek to place more or less of their products for sale in the market?

The standard suggestion in economics is that there is a positive relationship between the price of the product and supply. As the market price rises, so producers will wish to sell more of their product. There are two possible explanations available for this perceived relationship.

- *The profit-possibility explanation.* This explanation of the relationship between the price of the product and the amount of supply suggests that producers will increase their supply if market price rises, because there is the possibility of making greater profit. If everything else remains equal (*ceteris paribus*), then a higher selling price means more profit per product. If suppliers are motivated by profit then they will try to sell more and benefit from this higher profit potential. Equally, new firms will be interested in joining the market where there is an increased profit opportunity. This will also cause supply to increase over a longer period of time as these new firms then join the market and sell their products in it.

- *The increasing-costs explanation.* An alternative explanation of the positive relationship between the selling price of a product and the quantity that will be supplied is due to the so-called **law of diminishing returns**. It is often suggested that as production rises, then costs per unit of production will rise. If this is so, a higher market price will be required in order for it to be viable for producers to produce and sell more. Only with the higher price can the same level of profit per product sold be maintained. Higher selling prices thus permit a higher level of production and supply.

The law of diminishing returns suggests that as more and more of one resource (a variable factor of production) is added to a resource that does not vary in the short run (a fixed factor of production), then the extra production that is gained each time will diminish. There is less extra production for each further amount of resource that is added. This will mean that the cost of production per product will rise as more and more is produced.

The article from *The Daily Telegraph* about growing coffee and drugs in Colombia well illustrates this suggested relationship between the selling price of a product and the amount that may be produced and supplied for the market. The problem here is that there has been a persistent fall in the market price of coffee. This makes the growing of coffee beans less and less viable, especially when compared to the alternative of certain illegal drugs that have a far higher market price. The lower price of coffee is thus leading to a fall in the supply of that product.

Poverty and strife boost drug harvest in Colombia

JEREMY MCDERMOTT

In the Colombian Andes, the coffee plantations stretch up the sides of the mountains, dark-green bushes haphazardly covering the steep slopes.

Those who pick these bushes may be picking the world's finest coffee beans, but the owners of the smallholder plantations of Antioquia receive only 46p for a pound of arabica coffee from the national growers' federation. It costs 53p per pound to harvest and process the beans.

Farmer Gabriel Uribe, looking over his small plantation, sighs: 'It is not hard to do the maths. If we can sell the car and add that to our savings, at a push we have enough to last another year. After that we go under.'

Coffee prices have been falling on world markets for years. This week the price of arabica beans, the type grown in Colombia, fell to its lowest for nine years and that of poorer quality robusta beans to its lowest price for 35 years. Now many coffee farmers are turning to the only crops that offer them any chance of survival: coca and poppy, the

raw materials for cocaine and heroin.

The economics cannot compare: coffee just about breaks even if no extra fertiliser is pumped into the soil and the infrastructure of the farm is allowed to sink into neglect. The coca bushes flourish with no encouragement, producing a crop every 60 days; and the price of a pound of coca base is £300.

Octavio Asavedo, who has a typical seven-acre plantation in Antioquia, northern Colombia, says: 'We are beset on all sides. The gringos [Americans] are spraying chemicals on us anywhere they see a coca leaf, killing all plant life. The guerillas and paramilitaries are killing us. Now the international coffee market is killing our livelihood. We have no choice, it is drugs or joining the fighting.'

The statistics tell the story. America has sprayed defoliant on more than 125 000 acres of drug crops so far this year, yet Colombia has again registered an increase in the cultivated area, now estimated by the United Nations Drug Control Programme at 500 000 acres.

Adapted from *The Daily Telegraph*, 11 August 2001

The supply curve

As with demand, the relationship between the price of a product and the quantity of it supplied can be illustrated graphically with price on one axis and quantity supplied on the other axis. This is indicated in Figure 14.

The **supply curve** confirms the suggested relationship between price and quantity supplied explained above. As the selling price rises, so more supply is made available by producers. Thus the supply schedule slopes upwards from left to right.

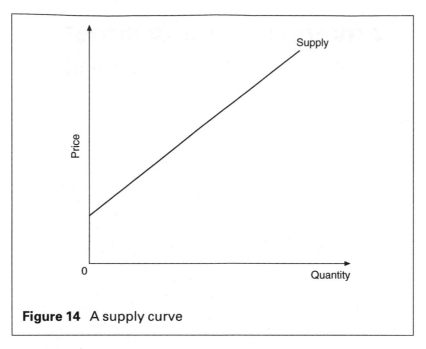

Figure 14 A supply curve

Changes in supply

There are three key factors that can cause the supply of a product to a market to change.

A change in the selling price

As has already been explained, if the selling price of the product changes, the suppliers will vary the amount of supply that is made available in a market.

Physical changes in supply

In some markets, supply may change due to a physical change in the supply of the product. This would typically be caused by changes in environmental and climatic conditions that go beyond the control of individual producers.

The clearest example of this sort of effect is within agriculture. The supply of an agricultural product is significantly determined by weather conditions. Crops may yield a high or a low harvest depending on the weather at certain times of the year. In these markets, supply can be greatly affected in this way (see *Chapter Six*).

This sort of effect is described in the article 'Farmers singing in the

Farmers singing in the rain

CREAN MIKE

Warm wet weather in the last two weeks has turned an already good season into a bumper one for many Canterbury farmers.

Fernside dryland sheep farmer Ian Stevenson said recent wet and warm weather had put the icing on the cake after the good spring. Contractors were flat out making hay, but he had managed to get two cuts done.

'Prices are good. If it stops raining we will cruise through to March. We have enough standing feed to keep the ewes going,' he said.

Warm, moist soil was perfect for planting winter feed crops. The only problem could be fly strike on sheep where farmers had not taken protective measures, Mr Stevenson said.

Grass and crop growth had been good. Farmers had made 'heaps' of hay, and some were into their second cut.

'A lot has been baled. Any surplus is a bonus. They have stored it in every nook and cranny, ready for whatever winter throws at us,' Ms Richardson, North Canterbury Federated Farmers president, said.

Adapted from *The Christchurch Press*, 4 January 2002

rain', about farming in New Zealand. Here, favourable conditions have led to an increase in supply.

Changes in the costs of production

Anything that causes a change in the cost of producing a product will have an impact upon supply. Any change in production costs will have an impact upon the profits of a firm and thus will affect the production decision.

If costs rise, then production will not be so profitable. Producers will cut back on their production. There will be less supplied at the same market price. On the other hand, if costs of production fall then production becomes more profitable. At the same price, suppliers thus wish to sell more of the product.

There are three main ways in which producers could find that their **costs of production** change.

- *A change in the cost of factors of production.* If any cost associated with the factors of production required to make a product changes, then the overall cost of production will change. This might be a change in the cost of raw materials. The world price of an important raw material used in the production of a particular good might significantly change the cost of producing that good. Another possibility could be a change in wage rates. If there is a large wage rise, perhaps due to a shortage of workers with a particular skill, then that will increase the costs of production. An increase in the productivity of workers would have the opposite effect. This will mean that each worker can produce more and thus that each product can be made with less labour cost.

- *A change in technology.* This can have a significant effect on the costs of production of a product. A breakthrough that might permit a new way of producing a product could significantly lower the cost of producing something of the same (or of a better) quality. One obvious example is the application of the silicon chip to many forms of production. Computerization has permitted machines to produce in a far more sophisticated fashion than was ever possible in the past. This has often led to the replacement of unskilled and semi-skilled labour with capital and has had a major impact upon the costs of production.

In the long run, the impact of new technology has probably had a greater effect than anything else in reducing costs of production and thus increasing supply. It is a trend that seems likely to continue with further future technological breakthroughs leading to a further significant reduction in costs. The article below about transportation suggests that incredible scientific developments could, for example, lead to large falls in the cost of travel.

Beam me up Scotty

CHARLES ARTHUR

It's teleportation, Jim, but not as Star Trek fans know it. A team of scientists in Australia have managed to 'teleport' a stream of information encoded in one laser beam and made it reappear in another beam a meter away using quantum physics.

The true value of the work will probably lie in creating super-secure communication channels for governments and financial institutions, as it is impossible to tap such quantum communications.

But Trekkies can live in hope: the team leader, Dr Pin Koy Lam, of the Australian National University in Canberra, reckons that in 'the next three to five years' someone will manage to teleport an atom. After that, teleporting an entire person such as Kirk or Spock would only be a question of repeating that feat with a billion billion billion atoms at once.

The Independent, 18 June 2002

Home care costs rocketing

JANE WALLACE

The sick and disabled face a huge increase in home care costs if new Government regulations become law.

The new regulations, which update the rules on employment agencies, are widely expected to force self-employed home care workers to become employees of the agency they get work through. This would require them to pay National Insurance contributions, sick pay and paid holidays. Currently this is not required as the home-carers are self-employed, and agents only receive a commission from their clients for putting them in touch with carers.

The measure could bump up the costs of providing care significantly, by some £14 000 a year in the worst cases, according to estimates from home care agency Able Community Care. These costs could be reduced, but not dramatically, if, as is hoped, the regulations also exempt all home care from value added tax (VAT).

Michael Gill, finance director for Able, says there could be a 60 per cent increase in costs if VAT exemption is not given, and 40 per cent if it is. The figures look bad.

Adapted from the *Daily Mail*, 30 March 2002

- *Government incentives.* The government may give negative or positive incentives for the production of a good or service that affects the costs of production. The most obvious examples of this are the use of **taxes and subsidies.** A tax on the sale of a product that has to be paid by the producer has the effect of increasing the cost of production. A subsidy that is paid to a firm for producing a good or service will be equivalent to lowering the cost of production. Both of these measures will thus have an impact upon supply.

An example of government taxation having an impact upon the cost of production of a service is given in the *Daily Mail* article about home care. Here, it seems that changes in tax rules and other regulations being introduced by the government will have a large impact upon the cost of supplying these services.

Changes in supply and the supply curve

Any change in supply can be illustrated using a supply curve diagram. There are two types of changes that need to be shown in different ways.

Firstly, there may be a change in supply due to a change in the price of the product. A change in the selling price of a product will cause a movement along the same supply schedule. This can be seen in Figure

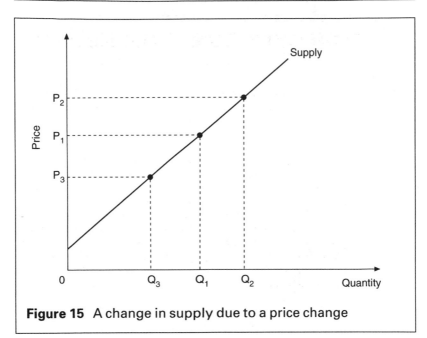

Figure 15 A change in supply due to a price change

15. The initial price is given as P_1 with an associated quantity supplied of Q_1. An increase in the selling price to P_2 causes the quantity supplied to rise to Q_2. This is referred to as an **extension of supply**. A fall in the selling price to P_3 causes the quantity supplied to fall to Q_3. That is called a **contraction of supply**.

Secondly, there may be a change in supply due to a non-price factor. Essentially, this means a change in the physical supply of the product or a change in the costs of production. Any such change will cause the supply curve to shift. This is illustrated in Figure 16. The initial supply schedule is S_1.

- There may then be something that causes the costs of production to fall (perhaps the government pays a new subsidy for the production of this particular product). This causes the supply schedule to move to the right as indicated by the curve S_2. This means that more is supplied (Q_2) at the same selling price.
- Alternatively there could be another factor that causes the costs of production to rise (perhaps the government introduces a new tax on the sale of this product). This causes the supply schedule to shift to the left as indicated by the curve S_3. This means that less is supplied (Q_3) at the same selling price.

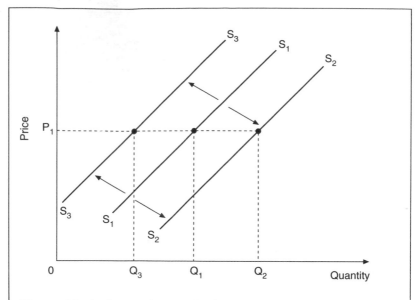

Figure 16 A change in supply due to a change in a non-price factor

Producer surplus

There is a producers equivalent to the consumers benefit (known as consumer surplus). **Producer surplus** refers to the amount that a producer receives for the production and sale of a product beyond the amount that the producer would have been prepared to sell the product for.

For example, a producer may have been prepared to put a product on to the market and sell it at a price of £10. However, the current market price for this product is £15. The producer is able to sell the product at this price. Thus the producer receives a surplus to the value of £5. This is called 'producer surplus'.

Producer surplus can be illustrated using a standard supply schedule as in Figure 17. The selling price for this product is P_1. This means that Q_1 of the product is supplied to the market. All products sold up to Q_1 then receive some producer surplus. Suppliers would have been prepared to sell them at a lower price. Thus the total value of the producer surplus is illustrated by the shaded area on the diagram.

Elasticity of supply

As with demand, the amount that supply will change due to a change in a particular factor can be measured. In the case of supply, there is only

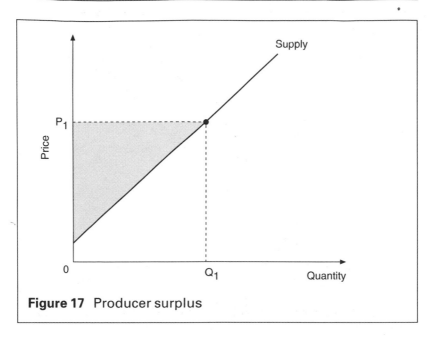

Figure 17 Producer surplus

one type of elasticity that is considered: **price elasticity of supply**. Thus any reference to elasticity of supply refers to this.

The value of the price elasticity of supply can be calculated by using the following equation:

Price elasticity of supply

$$= \frac{\text{percentage change in quantity supplied}}{\text{percentage change in price}}$$

The price elasticity of supply measures the responsiveness of the quantity supplied to a change in the selling price of the product. It indicates by how much the supply of a product will change due to a change in the price of that product.

The value of this will always be positive given the positive relationship between price and quantity supplied. The values can be divided up as follows:

- *A value between 0 and 1.* Any elasticity of supply measured within this range is described as inelastic. A change in price causes a relatively small change in supply.
- *A value of 1.* If elasticity of supply is measured to be exactly 1, then it is described as unitary. This means that a change in price causes an exactly proportionate change in quantity supplied.

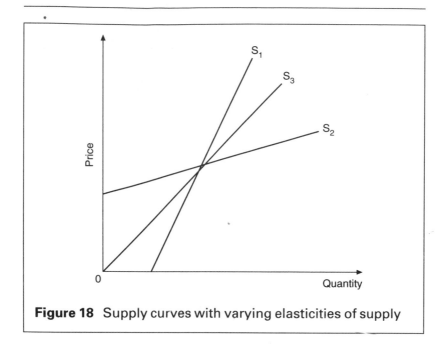

Figure 18 Supply curves with varying elasticities of supply

- *A value greater than 1.* Any elasticity of supply whose value is measured as greater than 1 is described as elastic. A change in price causes a relatively large change in the quantity supplied.

These different values for the price elasticity of supply can be illustrated on a supply curve diagram. Different types of supply schedules are associated with different values for the price elasticity of supply as seen in Figure 18.

- A supply schedule S_1 starting from the quantity axis illustrates a situation where quantity supplied changes less than proportionately compared to the change in price. It represents an inelastic supply.
- A supply schedule S_2 starting from the price axis illustrates that the quantity supplied changes more than proportionately compared to the change in price. It represents an elastic supply.
- A supply schedule S_3 starting from the origin illustrates that the quantity supplied changes exactly in proportion to the change in price. It represents a situation of unitary elasticity.

Factors influencing the price elasticity of supply
Several factors could determine the value of the price elasticity of supply for a product.

- *The existence of unsold stocks of the product.* If a producer has access to considerable amounts of unsold stocks of a product, then supply could be highly elastic. A higher price could quickly lead to significantly more of the product being supplied to the market.
- *The availability of appropriate factors of production.* If the factors of production required to produce the good or service are readily available, then production can respond to a change in price and supply may be elastic. This would mean more labour being readily available and spare capacity in factories with idle machines. If there is not such spare capacity then it will be very difficult for supply to respond to changes in the selling price of the product.
- *The time period involved.* The elasticity of supply will certainly be greater the longer the time period is. In the short run, it is not easy for producers to vary the amount that they can supply to the market. Production techniques cannot easily be changed. However, in the longer run suppliers can be much more flexible. New workers can be recruited and the means of production can be varied. A far greater supply response to a change in price is possible.

It is clearly of significance how great the price elasticity of supply of a product may be. For example, consumers may or may not be able to have access to the greater supply of a product that they demand, depending upon the price elasticity of supply. This will be considered further in the next chapter that looks at price determination. A simple example can be seen in *The Independent* article recommending that

Company car tax change looming

WILLIAM KAY

The Association of Chartered Certified Accountants (ACCA) warned last night that company car drivers should act now to combat the governments new carbon dioxide tax on car benefits due to take effect next month.

Chas Roy-Chowdury, ACCA's head of taxation, said: 'Generally speaking, it will be advisable to buy a car which has a smaller engine and is more fuel-efficient. This will help keep the tax charge to a minimum. I would advise those drivers whose companies are considering buying them new cars to choose carefully if they do not intend to pay above the flat-rate tax of fifteen per cent.'

Adapted from *The Independent*, 9 March 2002

firms should swap to purchasing cars with smaller engines for their employees in order to avoid a new tax on carbon dioxide. However, the extent to which firms will be able to do this will be dependent upon the ability of suppliers to respond. In other words, it will depend upon the price elasticity of supply.

KEY WORDS	
Producers	Taxes and subsidies
Law of diminishing marginal returns	Extension of supply
	Contraction of supply
Supply curve	Producer surplus
Costs of production	Price elasticity of supply

Further reading
Bamford, C. (ed.), Unit 1, section 1 in *Economics for AS*, Cambridge University Press, 2000.

Grant, S., Chapter 10 in *Stanlake's Introductory Economics*, 7th edn, Longman, 2000.

Grant, S. and Vidler, C., Part 1, Unit 7 in *Economics in Context*, Heinemann Educational, 2000.

Parkin, M. Powell, M. and Matthews, K., Chapter 4 in *Economics*, 4th edn, Pearson Educational, 2000.

Useful website
Agricultural markets: http://netec.mcc.ac.uk/
Click on WOPEC (Data about electronic working papers) to find papers and journal articles.

Essay topics
1. (a) Explain why supply curves slope up from left to right. [8 marks]
   (b) Discuss three causes of an increase in the supply of wheat. [12 marks]

2. (a) Explain the main influences on price elasticity of supply. [10 marks]
   (b) A product is found to have a price elasticity of demand of −0.6 and a price elasticity of supply of 2.5. Explain the significance of these figures for its producers. [10 marks]

Data response question
This task is based on a question set by Edexcel in January 2002. Read the following article, which is adapted from *The Economist* of 25 November 2000. Then answer the questions that follow.

European steel

Just outside Dunkirk, on France's northern border, is Sollac, one of Europe's biggest and most efficient steel plants. Owned by Usinor, France's biggest steel company, Sollac has its own port, railway and a 55km (35-mile) road network. In one continuous process, it takes raw iron ore and coal from all over the world and turns them into top-quality rolls of steel. Visitors to Sollac cannot fail to be impressed by its scale. Its output this year will be six million metric tonnes.

Europe has six of the worlds ten biggest steel companies. They are relatively recent products of mergers between once state-owned companies. Privatized during the early 1990s, they faced particularly tough markets because of low-cost new entrants in Asia. The break-up of the Soviet Union, which had not previously exported steel to the West, added 40 million tonnes of capacity to an already stretched industry. The European steel companies responded to this by merging into bigger, tougher cross-border corporations, and by expanding into new markets overseas, in particular Latin America. They also became more efficient, gaining economies of scale, and between 1970 and 1996 the number of workers employed in the European steel industry fell from 725 000 to 220 000.

The result of all this cost-cutting is that Europe's steel companies remain competitive when measured against global rivals. But Sollac, and other steel mills like it, operate in a desperately bleak environment. The fear is that the world economy is slowing down. Demand for steel is strongly influenced by the construction and car industries. In Europe, demand from these customers is slipping. Steel prices have been falling in response, by seven per cent on average since August. Steel stocks have begun to swell.

The impact on steel makers will be painful. Cuts announced in production have come too late and are too little to make much difference, at least until well into next year.

There is little that steel firms can do to improve matters for themselves. Both their suppliers and customers have been faster to merge than they have, and are generally larger and more powerful, limiting the steel firms' room for manoeuvre. Furthermore, raw material costs have been rising, as a result of higher oil prices pushing up the costs of running coking plants.

1. Explain the term 'elasticity of supply' and how it is measured.
   [2 marks]
2. Using a supply and demand diagram, analyse why steel prices had been falling 'by seven per cent on average since August'.
   [6 marks]
3. With reference to the passage and other knowledge, analyse the likely impact of lower steel prices on:
   (a) steel producers   [3 marks]
   (b) the market for steel *substitutes*.   [3 marks]

Chapter Five

Price determination

'It is not that pearls fetch a higher price because men have dived for them; but on the contrary, men dive for them because they fetch a high price.'
Richard Whately, *Introductory Lectures on Political Economy*

Prices are fundamental to our economy. We frequently enquire as to the prices of different products. We pass comment upon whether we deem particular prices to be high or low. In economics, we recognize the vital role that prices play in allocating scarce resources. Depending on the price of products, we do or do not demand them. This dictates the amount of resources that are then used to produce each product.

Prices are central to our economic system. The crucial question that this chapter seeks to address is what determines those prices. What determines the market price of a product? Why are some prices higher than other prices? Why do some prices rise while other prices fall? According to economists, it is all down to supply and demand.

Equilibrium price

Of all the crucial suggestions made by the subject of economics, the suggestion that the combined forces of supply and demand determine prices is perhaps the most fundamental of all. In the history of economic thought, economists long wrestled with what it was that was truly responsible for prices being what they were. The final answer was seen to be that it was the combination of supply and demand for a product that determined its price. In the words of the famous economist Alfred Marshall, it was 'the twin blades' of supply and demand, like the two blades of a pair of scissors, that together determined price.

In order to understand this vital suggestion, we must combine the demand described in *Chapter Two* of this book with the supply considered in *Chapter Four*. This is best done with a diagram that combines a demand curve with a supply curve, as indicated in Figure 19.

The theory of price determination suggests that it is where demand is equal to supply that the price of the product will be given. This is referred to as the **equilibrium price**. Equilibrium price is the point where the supply of a product is equal to the demand for that product. It is the price that does not tend to change. All other prices will vary,

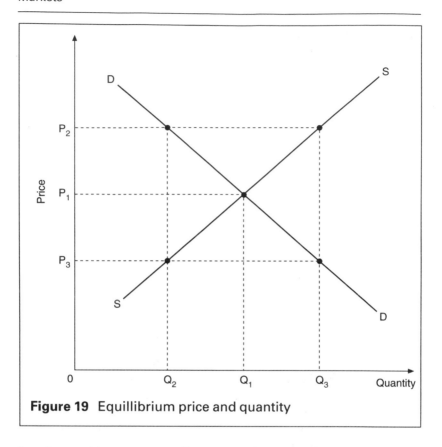

Figure 19 Equillibrium price and quantity

but the equilibrium price will stay put. The reason for this can be seen in Figure 19.

The equilibrium price is shown at P_1, which has an associated equilibrium quantity of Q_1. Without anyone planning it, that is the price that will exist in the market. The best way to understand this is to consider what happens in the market if price is not at P_1 where supply is equal to demand.

At a price of P_2, above the equilibrium price, supply is not equal to demand. At this higher price, producers wish to supply a larger amount, Q_3. However, as this is a high price, consumers demand only a small amount, Q_2. Supply is thus greater than demand. This has a clear implication: a **surplus** is created. There are more of the products available to be sold than there are consumers willing to purchase them. This situation is not likely to persist. Suppliers will not simply retain these stocks of unsold products: they will act to sell them (and thus make money on them). The way to sell them is to alter price in order to increase sales. The market price thus falls and the surplus is cleared. P_2 is not an equilibrium price. Where supply is greater than demand, price will fall.

An alternative price is P_3. This is lower than the equilibrium price of P_1. At this lower price, demand is at a high level, Q_3. However, owing to the low price, producers wish to supply only a low quantity, Q_2. Thus demand is greater than supply at P_3. There is a **shortage**. More consumers wish to purchase the products than there are available. This situation will not persist. Profit-maximizing suppliers will realize that they are running out of products while there are still plenty of willing consumers. They thus recognize a profit possibility if they change price. They can see that they could still sell all of their products if price were higher given the excess demand. Suppliers thus increase their prices. A price where demand is greater than supply will not persist, it will rise.

There is thus only one price that will not tend to change. The equilibrium price is where supply equals demand. Only at this price is there no incentive for suppliers either to increase or to decrease price.

Examples can be found where governments do not allow prices to adjust in the way predicted in normal markets. In these cases, price does not move to its equilibrium level:

* *The European Union's* **Common Agricultural Policy.** One aspect of this policy has been to guarantee certain **minimum prices** for certain agricultural products. This is similar to maintaining price at P_2 in Figure 19. Governments do not allow price to fall to the equilibrium. The result is that surpluses of agricultural products persist and they have to be purchased by governments.
* *Fixed low prices in so-called command economies.* In the former government-controlled command economies of eastern Europe, prices were often fixed at a low level for many products. This can be likened to preserving prices at P_3 in Figure 19. The result is that there was often a shortage of various products. Large **queues** for these products could thus be witnessed and **black markets** with higher prices often existed.

With this understanding of how prices are determined, it becomes possible to analyse the price of any product in terms of the different forces of supply and demand that exist for it. This can be seen in the work of Gerrard and Dobson in explaining football transfer fees (see the following box). The key factors they identify dictate the supply of, and demand for, footballers – and thus determine their price.

Economists can predict football transfer fees

Transfer fees in the English Football League are highly predictable, according to Dr Bill Gerrard and Dr Steve Dobson in a presentation to the Scottish Centennial Conference in Stirling in April 1997. In their wide-ranging analysis, they found:

- The quality of the individual player is a key factor in determining his transfer fee. This includes his position, age, domestic and international experience, career goal-scoring rate and current form as measured by league appearances and goals scored in the season prior to transfer.
- International experience is particularly important.
- Transfer fees are also determined by the characteristics of the buying and selling clubs. Premier League clubs are prepared to bid around thirty per cent more than Division One clubs for any given player.
- Buying clubs that are competing to win the league, gain promotion or avoid relegation pay a premium for players in March when the transfer deadline occurs.

Source: Adapted from B. Gerrard and S. Dobson, 'Testing for rent-sharing in football transfer fees: evidence from the English Football League', 1997

Changes in price

If the equilibrium price is determined by supply and demand, then changes in the price of a product must be due to changes in supply and/or demand. There are four possible cases, each of which can be understood with an appropriate supply and demand diagram.

An increase in demand

Figure 20 illustrates the effect of an increase in demand. The starting position is where supply equals demand at price P_1 and quantity Q_1. Something then causes demand to increase – for example, an increase in consumers income for a normal good. This causes the demand schedule to shift to the right (D_2). This means that price P_1 cannot persist. At this price, demand is now greater than supply. There is thus upward pressure on the market price. Price rises until it reaches the new higher equilibrium at P_2.

A decrease in demand

Figure 21 illustrates the effect of a decrease in demand. The starting equilibrium price is at P_1 where supply is equal to demand.

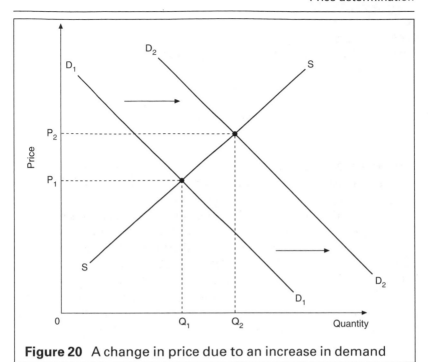

Figure 20 A change in price due to an increase in demand

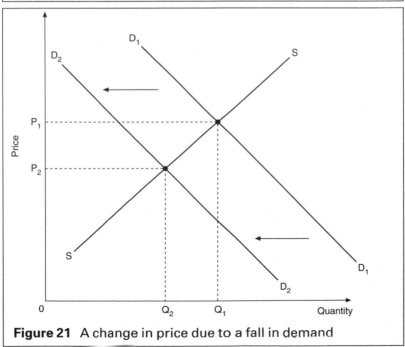

Figure 21 A change in price due to a fall in demand

The equilibrium quantity is Q_1. Demand then decreases for this product. The price of a substitute product may have fallen so that consumers transfer their demand away from this product. This causes the demand schedule to shift to the left (D_2). Price P_1 can no longer persist. At this price, supply is now greater than demand and there is a surplus of the product. Suppliers thus reduce price until the new equilibrium price of P_2 is reached.

An increase in supply

Figure 22 illustrates an increase in supply. The initial equilibrium price is P_1 where supply is equal to demand, and the associated quantity is Q_1. There is then an increase in supply of the product. This may have been caused by an increase in labour productivity that means that the same number of workers can now make more of the product. This reduces the cost of producing each product and thus increases supply. This is indicated by a rightward movement of the supply curve (S_2). Price P_1 is now no longer the equilibrium price. Supply is greater than demand at this price. Suppliers will thus reduce price until the equilibrium is restored at the lower equilibrium price of P_2.

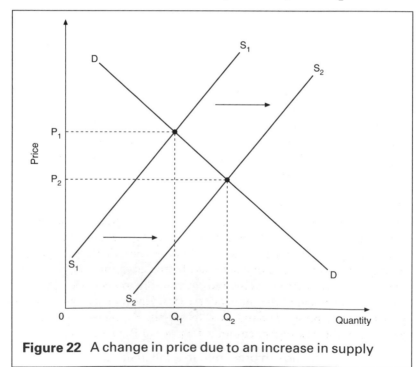

Figure 22 A change in price due to an increase in supply

Britain attacks $51BN US farm subsidies

DAVIS WASTELL AND FRANCIS ELLIOT

President Bush's decision to sanction substantial new subsidies for American farmers has provoked howls of protest in Britain and Europe over 'hypocritical' United States trade policy.

Farmers in America are to receive increases in state aid of up to 67 per cent under a bill to be passed into law by President Bush tomorrow.

A European official in Washington said 'we're supposed to be working towards another world trade round, which the President says he supports. One of the key elements, which we have agreed, is a cut in agricultural subsidy. The fear is that this will be exploited by those opposed to reform'.

Growers of soya beans, dairy farmers and producers of wheat, cotton and rice in prairie and southern states stand to gain billions of extra tax dollars over the next decade following Mr Bush's decision to support the increase.

'There is a real likelihood that this farm support will trigger a downward spiral' said one Washington official. 'It will encourage farmers to produce more and lead to even lower prices, which will then trigger higher subsidies and an even bigger bill'.

The Daily Telegraph, 12 May 2002

Anything that could cause a rightward movement of the supply schedule could cause this effect. For example, any form of government subsidy will work in this way. A subsidy will have the effect of reducing the costs of production and thus causing a rightward movement of the supply schedule. This is the effect of the US farm subsidies that are discussed in *The Daily Telegraph* article above.

A decrease in supply

Figure 23 indicates what happens if there is a decrease in supply. As before, the starting equilibrium price is P_1 and the quantity Q_1. At this point, supply is equal to demand. Supply then decreases, possibly owing to the imposition of a sales tax by the government. This causes the costs of production to rise and thus supply to decrease. There is a leftward movement of the supply curve (S_2). Given this, P_1 will not now persist. At this point, demand exceeds supply. Suppliers will thus raise prices until the new higher equilibrium price of P_2 is reached.

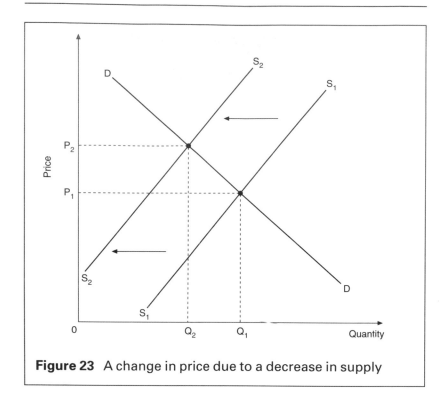

Figure 23 A change in price due to a decrease in supply

Examples of price changes

All price changes can be understood as either one of, or a combination of, the above possibilities. The analysis of **commodity price** changes suggests supply and demand changes are causing changes in different commodity prices. For example, the *Financial Times* article suggests that the price of cotton is expected to rise due to an increase in demand. Wool prices rose due to fears over a fall in supply, but lower demand in the future could have the opposite effect. Higher demand and restricted supply for rubber are both likely to push up its price (see also *Chapter Six*).

The *Daily Telegraph* report about falling computer prices indicates one key factor that was pushing down the price of computers at the end of the year 2000. Demand had fallen. Surpluses had thus been created and suppliers were being forced to cut their prices. This is precisely as suggested in Figure 21.

Price rise forecast for raw materials

ADRIENNE ROBERTS

The worst is over for most raw material prices, according to the London-based Economist Intelligence Unit (EIU). 'Fibres and natural rubber will prove the chief beneficiaries as the global economy picks up [implying rising demand], although the base metals segment will also return to positive price growth,' said Matthew Parry, EIU commodities editor.

The EIU's industrial raw materials price index of nine hard commodities, which fell 9.8 per cent last year, is forecast to climb 5.5 per cent in 2002, speeding up in 2003 with year-on-year growth of 11.2 per cent.

Fibres are expected to climb 10.4 per cent in 2002. Cotton prices are expected to gain from a general improvement in economic sentiment.

Wool prices, which rose sharply in the first two months of this year on supply concerns, are expected to remain strong this year. But the EIU thinks demand could weaken next year as consumers eventually switch to cheaper substitute fibres.

Natural rubber, which fell 10.2 per cent last year, is expected to rise 8.5 per cent. Key sources of support include demand from China's growing automotive and tyre industries, and the recent progress by the three main producers in establishing a cartel.

Adapted from the *Financial Times*, 27 March 2002

Price changes and elasticity

The price elasticities of supply and demand are important factors in considering the effect on price of a change in supply or demand. The *amount* that price will alter due to a change in demand or supply will depend upon the price elasticity of demand or supply.

A change in demand

We know that an increase in demand will cause the equilibrium price of a product to rise. However, we do not know by how much it will rise. That will depend upon the price elasticity of supply. This is illustrated in Figure 24.

There has been an increase in demand indicated by the rightward movement of the demand curve from D_1 to D_2. This means that the equilibrium price of P_1 will not persist. However, the extent of the price rise generated depends upon the elasticity of supply. If supply is

Computer prices plummet

Andy Goldberg

There has never been a better time to buy PCs as computer manufacturers and retailers are forced to discount their prices despite the typical Christmas rush. The price cuts are affecting most of the world's largest computer manufacturers, such as Apple and Compaq.

Sales in America were poor in October and November, showing a twelve per cent decline compared with last year. This month the figures have been down by nearly thirty per cent. The biggest bargains are in America, but they are expected to spread to the UK and the rest of Europe.

The price cuts can be linked to various factors, largely a belief that the PC market in America has reached saturation point – anyone who wants a computer already has one. Many people are buying mobile phones and high-tech gadgets such as electronic organizers, rather than PCs.

In previous years, many computer owners would decide to upgrade to new models at Christmas. However, if you bought a new computer in the last few years, it is probably perfectly capable of performing the functions you want, such as email and surfing the net. Kevin Knox, an analyst at the research group Gartner, said: 'This is turning out to be much worse than we initially reported. You are going to see more drastic measures. By Christmas you could see people giving PCs away.'

Adapted from *The Daily Telegraph*, 14 December

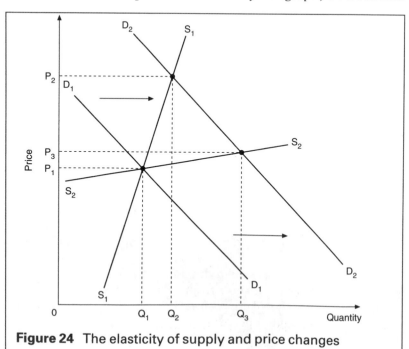

Figure 24 The elasticity of supply and price changes

inelastic, as with supply schedule S_1, then price increases significantly to P_2 as the quantity supplied can respond little. However, if supply is elastic, as with supply curve S_2, then price rises only a little to P_3 as the quantity supplied can vary considerably.

An inelastic supply can mean that any change in demand can have a large impact upon price. This can be seen in the housing market. If demand rises, supply cannot respond at all readily: the housing stock is largely fixed in the short run. The supply schedule is similar to S_1. Thus there is a large price effect (see also *Chapter Six*).

A decrease in supply

Figure 25 illustrates the impact of different elasticities of demand resulting from a change in supply. A reduction in supply is indicated by the leftward movement of the supply curve from S_1 to S_2. This will cause price to increase from its initial equilibrium of P_1. However, the extent to which it will increase will depend upon the elasticity of demand.

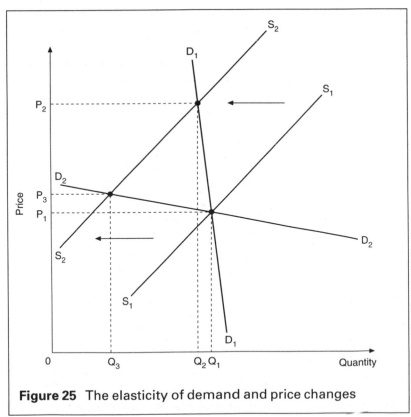

Figure 25 The elasticity of demand and price changes

- If demand is price inelastic, as with the demand schedule D_1, then there will be a large price rise. The quantity demanded varies little and price rises considerably to P_2.
- On the other hand, if demand is price elastic, as with the demand curve D_2, then price will rise only a little to P_3. There will be a significant change in the quantity demanded.

This information could be highly significant for the government when considering the taxation of different products. If the government wishes to use taxes on products to raise revenue and not to have a major negative impact on the industry, then it is much better to tax products with inelastic demands. The tax causes the supply schedule to shift to the left as in Figure 25. If demand is inelastic, as with curve D_1, then demand remains high for the product despite the tax, and so high revenue is raised. Government taxes on petrol, tobacco and alcohol could all be understood in this light – they are all products with relatively inelastic demands. The government places a large tax upon them and raises a lot of revenue from the taxes.

The operation of **OPEC**, the oil exporting **cartel**, in controlling the world supply of oil can also be understood in this way. If oil is deemed

Oil prices to soar as OPEC cuts output

MARY FAGAN

OPEC is poised this week to agree production cuts of up to 2m barrels a day, fuelling fears about a renewed surge in oil prices and a repeat of last year's fuel crisis which threatened to bring the country to a halt.

The likely OPEC cuts of between 1.5m and 2m barrels a day, to be decided at a meeting in Vienna on Wednesday, are higher than had been hoped and could push petrol prices up in advance of a general election in the UK. The OPEC nations aim to stabilize crude oil prices, which have fallen recently thirty per cent from highs last year of about $32 a barrel, at about $25.

But prices have already risen in anticipation of production cutbacks and there are fears that they could settle at $28 or more. As a rough rule of thumb, every $1 on a barrel of crude translates in the UK to an increase in the price at the pump of just under 0.5p. One industry insider said: 'An increase in the price of crude will inevitably result at some point in an increase at the pump.'

OPEC fears a repetition of what happened in 1998, when prices fell to $10 a barrel because of high oil stocks and a surplus in supply.

Adapted from *The Daily Telegraph*, 14 January 2001

to have a price inelastic demand (there are no close substitutes for certain important operations involving the use of oil) then restricting supply will have a major impact upon the world price of oil. This is what the *The Daily Telegraph* article suggests OPEC was attempting to do at the beginning of 2001.

KEY WORDS

Equilibrium price	Queues
Surplus	Black markets
Shortage	Commodity price
Common Agricultural Policy	OPEC
Minimum prices	Cartel

Further reading
Bamford, C. (ed.), Unit 1, section 1 in *Economics for AS*, Cambridge University Press, 2000.
Grant, S., Chapter 11 in *Stanlake's Introductory Economics*, 7th edn, Longman, 2000.
Grant, S. and Vidler, C., Part 1, Unit 8 in *Economics in Context*, Heinemann Educational, 2000.
Munday, S., Chapter 3 in *Markets and Market Failure*, Heinemann Educational, 2000.

Useful websites
- Oil market: www.oilprices.com
- Computer market: www.computerprices.co.uk

Essay topics
1. Many homes in the UK now own a personal computer (PC) and the price of PCs has fallen in recent years. Use supply and demand analysis to show how an economist might explain this price fall.
   [20 marks]
   [OCR, November 1999]

2. Explain, using demand and supply diagrams, the effect on the market for new cars of:
   (a) a rise in incomes; [5 marks]
   (b) a subsidy given to car producers; [5 marks]
   (c) a fall in the price of second-hand cars; [5 marks]

(d) a rise in the wages of car workers not matched by an increase in their productivity. [5 marks]

Data response question

This task is based on a question set by AQA in June 2001. Study Figure A and the two extracts (the second extract is adapted from the *Financial Times* of 22 February 2000) and then answer the questions that follow.

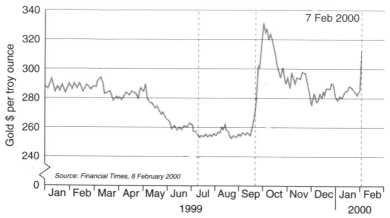

Figure A The price of gold on the London Metal market

The price of gold

The price of gold, like the price of other commodities, is determined by supply and demand. But unlike many other commodities, both supply of, and demand for, gold are affected significantly by the activities of governments. In May 1999, the British government announced that more than half the UK's gold reserves would be sold over future months. This was followed by similar announcements by other European governments.

But in September 1999, the European governments changed their policy, announcing a limit to the sale of gold from reserves. Then, early in February 2000, a number of major North American and South African gold mining companies decided to reduce the supply of newly mined gold on to the market.

The demand for jewellery is increasing by twenty-three per cent. This is another factor which may affect the price of gold in future months.

The price of palladium

The precious metal palladium occurs in the same group of metallic ores as platinum. A mining company can sometimes increase production of palladium by reducing production of platinum, and vice versa, but this requires time and a very heavy investment in new capital equipment. Russia is the world's leading producer of palladium. South Africa is in second place, but a long way behind.

Demand for palladium has increased rapidly in recent years. Unlike gold and platinum, the demand for palladium is restricted to industrial uses. The metal's main use is in catalytic converters built into the exhaust systems of automobiles to reduce pollution. Currently no other metal can be used for this purpose. However, the major car producers are confident that substitutes can be developed in the long term.

Supplies of the metal are increasingly tight as a result of the Russian government's decision not to release palladium from its stockpile. In conditions of rapidly rising demand, selling from stocks traditionally plugs the gap between demand (currently eight million ounces) and mine production (around five and a half million ounces). Also, the Russia government recently imposed an export tax on the metal. This caused the price of palladium to surge in just one day on the London market by nearly twenty per cent to $800 an ounce. The metal's price was in the $300 to $400 range in 1999.

1. Describe the changes in the price of gold shown in Figure A over the period from January 1999 to February 2000.   [5 marks]

2. With the help of a supply and demand diagram, explain briefly how an increase in jewellery demand mentioned in the first extract may affect the price of gold.   [4 marks]

3. Making use of the information in the second extract, explain why both the demand for, and the supply of, palladium are likely to be more price elastic in the long run than in the short run.
    [6 marks]

Chapter Six

Applications of demand and supply analysis

'The Euro yesterday gave up some of the gains that it had made against the pound and the dollar on the first day of trading after the introduction of notes and coins.'

The Daily Telegraph, 4 January 2002

The **euro**, which became the currency of twelve EU member states on 1 January 2002, is likely to quickly establish itself as a world reserve currency, along with the US dollar. On 4 January, one euro was worth £0.6245 and $US0.9003 – we can now expect fluctuations to be quoted daily in the media. Like any international currency, this rate will be determined by the forces of demand and supply in the international exchange markets.

Other examples of markets where demand and supply applications are important include:

- the **labour market,** where **wages** are determined by the demand and supply of labour
- the **money market,** where the **rate of interest** is determined by the demand and supply of money
- agricultural and **commodity markets,** where prices are subject to fluctuation due to demand and supply conditions
- the **housing market,** which is an unusual application of the principles of demand and supply analysis.

In all cases the basic determination of prices (which generally includes wages and the rate of interest) is through the respective forces of demand and supply. It should be stressed, though, that this is how these markets work in theory – in practice, because of market failures, some form of intervention is required to produce a better allocation of resources. (See *Markets and Market Failure* by S. Munday, Heinemann Educational, 2000 for more details.)

The foreign exchange market

The buying and selling of international currencies takes place on the **foreign exchange market.** Every day there is a need for the buying and selling of currencies such as the pound, the US dollar, the euro, the

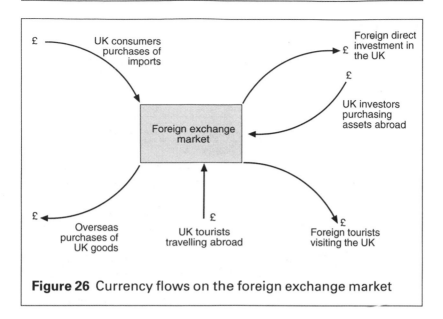

Figure 26 Currency flows on the foreign exchange market

Japanese yen and so on. Figure 26 shows the main flows in this market from a UK perspective.

- **Imports** and **exports** of goods. Importers of goods into the UK will use pounds to buy the currency of the country where they are purchasing goods. This act provides a supply of pounds on to the foreign exchange market. Similarly, the demand for pounds is created by those buying products from the UK – their own currencies are used to buy pounds in the foreign exchange market.
- **International tourism.** UK tourists travelling abroad need to buy international currencies. For this, they use pounds, purchasing other currencies from this supply of funds. In turn, visitors to the UK demand pounds to fund their stay – for this purpose, they will supply their own currencies and buy pounds through the foreign exchange market.
- **Foreign direct investment.** Companies investing in the UK require pounds to purchase assets in the UK, whereas UK companies investing in the rest of the EU, the USA or the rest of the world will have to exchange pounds for other international currencies.

International currency flows therefore are generated through trade in goods and services and through short and long-term capital flows. Foreign direct investment is long term in its nature, in contrast to 'hot

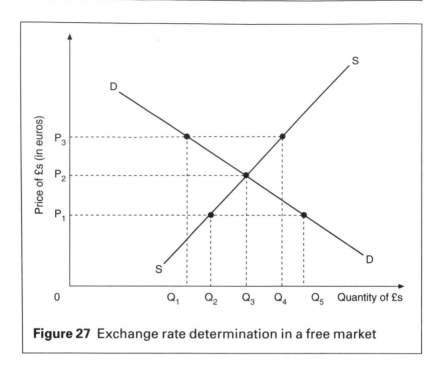

Figure 27 Exchange rate determination in a free market

money' flows which tend to move between economies in search of the highest returns.

In a free market, the value of the **exchange rate** is determined simply by the forces of supply and demand. The exchange rate is therefore a price, where supply and demand clears. Figure 27 shows the supply and demand for pounds on the foreign exchange market. For simplicity, we will illustrate this with reference only to the relationship between the pound and the euro.

- The demand curve for pounds is like any other demand curve – it slopes downwards from left to right, indicating that when the price of the pound is high in terms of euros (P_3 for example), UK goods and services are relatively expensive in the 'euro zone'. As a consequence, demand for British imports in these countries will be low. Fewer pounds are demanded on the foreign exchange market and the value of the pound falls against the euro. In turn, euro zone consumers can get more pounds for their euros, so more pounds are demanded.
- The supply curve for pounds is upward-sloping from left to right. When the value of the pound against the euro is low (P_1 for

example), euro zone goods are relatively more expensive than domestically produced goods in the UK. Consequently, fewer pounds will be supplied to the foreign exchange market; as the value of the pound rises, then more pounds are supplied as more euro zone goods become affordable to UK consumers. Equilibrium in the market is reached at P_2, where the demand for and supply of pounds are equal.

So, if a currency is *overvalued* in the foreign exchange market, there is an excess of it and market forces will result in a fall in its price. If a currency is *undervalued*, then more is being demanded than is being supplied; consequently its price will rise.

Any significant change in supply or demand for a currency will cause a **depreciation** or **appreciation** in its exchange rate. A depreciation is represented by a downward shift in the demand curve for a currency; an appreciation is shown by an upward shift in the supply curve (see Figure 28).

When the value of the pound against the euro depreciates, then its price falls from P_2 to P_1.

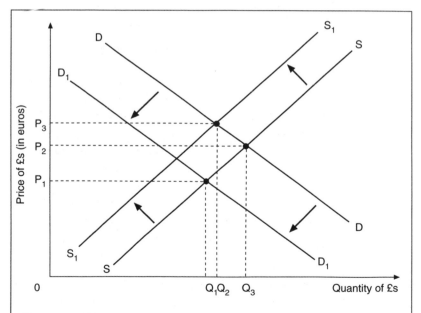

Figure 28 The effects on the supply and demand curves of depreciation or appreciation in sterling exchange rate

This can occur for various reasons, including:

- a fall in demand for UK goods and services in the euro zone
- fewer euro zone tourists visiting the UK
- a reduction in euro zone investment in the UK economy, probably due to a loss of confidence in future economic prospects.

One of the most significant currency depreciations in recent years has been that of the Japanese yen, especially against the US dollar. At the end of 2001 the yen had tumbled to a new low of 132 yen per dollar (see *The Daily Telegraph* article).

This collapse of the previously strong Japanese currency is symptomatic of the problems currently being experienced by the Japanese economy, largely in the aftermath of the south-east Asian currency crisis of 1996. With high unemployment, and practically zero

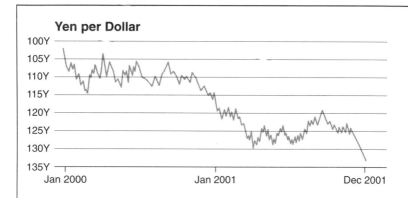

Yen per Dollar

The yen tumbled to a three-and-a-half year low in London yesterday as the recession in Japan deepened with industrial output last month falling to its lowest levels for fourteen years.

The dollar, which has appreciated by more than 6 per cent against the yen this month, rose to Y132.08 at one stage yesterday, before closing in London at Y131.39, against Y131.025 on Monday and Y130.85 overnight in New York. A slide in motor vehicle production – a legacy of the September 11 terrorist attacks on America – was largely blamed for the 1.8 per cent drop in output between October and November, the third monthly slippage in a row.

Retail sales in November were down for the eighth successive month, while construction orders dropped almost 7 per cent and housing starts 1.2 per cent.

Adapted from *The Daily Telegraph*, 28 December 2001

inflation and interest rates, the Japanese economy continues in recession. The latest fall in the foreign exchange value of the yen has been precipitated by falling industrial output and the sluggish demand for Japanese exports in the USA. The yen's depreciation should in theory make Japanese exports relatively cheaper, stimulating domestic production and employment.

Alternatively, an appreciation of the pound against the euro (an increase from P_2 to P_3 on Figure 28), can occur as a consequence of:

- a decrease in demand for euro area imports in the UK
- more UK tourists taking holidays in the UK rather than in euro zone countries
- a decrease in the volume of investment by UK companies in the euro zone.

When a currency operates in the ways described above then the foreign exchange rate is said to be **freely floating**. Under this system, the exchange rate is determined purely by market forces. Such a system has various advantages, not least as it means governments are able to pursue other policy objectives without having to worry too much about their exchange rate and balance of payments. The automatic adjustment mechanism inherent in such a system can assist economies faced with inflation and unemployment problems.

Despite the seemingly obvious advantage, freely floating exchange rate regimes have various serious disadvantages. For example, where exchange rates fluctuate, an extra risk is added to international trade transactions – a sudden fluctuation in the exchange rate could result in massive losses or greater profits being earned, adding to uncertainty. It should also be recognized that a depreciating exchange rate can fuel rather than correct inflation – imports increase in price as a consequence of the fall in the exchange rate, so increasing rather than decreasing domestic inflation.

For these reasons, most exchange rate regimes in operation tend to favour some degree of intervention so that the exchange rate is managed or pegged between upper and lower limits. This is the underlying principle on which the new euro operates.

The labour market

All students of economics will at some time become part of the labour market. Indeed, some may already be participating through part-time employment whilst still at school or college. For this market, the key question that economic analysis seeks to resolve is why some workers get paid more than others. And why is it that some people with exceptional talent are very highly paid? The simple answer is that it all depends upon the supply and demand for labour.

The demand for labour is a **derived demand**. By this we mean that a firms demand for labour is due to its decision to produce certain goods and services. Labour is therefore demanded not for its own sake but because it is essential for the production of a whole range of goods and services. The firms decision to hire labour is based on the value of the worker's **marginal revenue product**, that is the amount of revenue generated through the employment of one additional worker. Where the value of the marginal product is above the prevailing wage rate then businesses will hire that worker. This process will persist until a point is reached where the marginal revenue product equals the wage rate that is being paid. Beyond this point, no further workers will be employed. The marginal revenue product curve therefore is a firms demand curve for labour.

The supply of labour is best seen in terms of the total number of hours that labour is able and willing to provide at a particular wage rate. The general principles of supply, introduced in *Chapter Four*, apply in the labour market, although it is important to remember that we are now dealing with people and their willingness (or otherwise) to participate in the market depending on the wage rate that they are being offered for their services.

If we consider the supply of labour to a firm, then the supply curve can be determined through aggregating all of the individual supply curves of workers willing to be employed by this firm. This supply curve is usually upward-sloping throughout, indicating that more workers will be willing to supply their labour as the wage rate rises (see Figure 29). The slope of the supply curve is measured by the elasticity of supply of labour – Figure 29 shows two different supply curves, one inelastic (L_1) and the other elastic (L_2).

There are various possible reasons for this difference. An obvious one is the skills required to carry out a particular occupation; in general, the more skills required the more inelastic will be the supply of labour. Similarly, where extensive education and training is needed to do a job, supply will be more inelastic than say in the case of a road sweeper where no particular skills or education and training are needed. L_2 in Figure 29 is likely to be the supply curve of labour to an industry where there is a plentiful supply of labour and where no particular skills or training are needed.

The price of labour, the wage, is no different to any other price in so far as it is determined in a free market by demand and supply. The market therefore clears at the equilibrium wage. This is shown in

Figure 29 Labour supply curves of varying elasticities

Figure 30.

Like any market, the labour market is dynamic and any change in the demand or in the supply of labour will change the equilibrium wage. Take the healthcare market as an example.

- The *demand* for qualified nurses in the National Health Service (NHS) and in the private sector continues to increase, partly as a consequence of an ageing population. By 2004, for example, it has been estimated that a further 20 000 nurses will be required in the NHS compared with 2001. The effect of this on the market is to shift the demand curve to the right, resulting in an increase in the wages of all nurses. The extent of the increase in wages will be dependent upon the elasticity of supply (see Figure 31).
- The *supply* of qualified nurses in the NHS has increased in recent years through the recruitment of nurses from outside the UK. The effect of this is to shift the supply curve to the right. In theory, this could actually result in a reduction in the wages of all nurses. In reality, this will not happen owing to the current shortage and the uproar there would be if this were to happen. Again, the extent of the change in the equilibrium wage rate is dependent upon the

Wanted – waiters, teachers and nurses

The supply of labour in certain types of occupation lags behind demand, creating a situation of shortage. In theory, the labour market should adjust to this situation through more people being willing to work in these occupations. Increasingly, to meet this shortfall, the additional labour is from outside the UK. The examples below are typical of how the market has responded in three occupations where the supply of labour has been below demand.

Joining the foreign legion

The Daily Telegraph, 15 August 1998

A new breed of young waiters has invaded Britain ... young foreigners seeking to earn a living while they travel around. There is a shortage of waiting staff in London. In May, there were at least 30 000 unfilled vacancies in the hospitality industry in London. More and more waiting staff are foreign and young. Briton's do not like serving each other ... consequently many staff in the capital's hotels and restaurants come from other parts of the EU, and from Cuba, South Africa, Australia and eastern Europe. These young aspiring members of the foreign legion seem much happier to work long hours, for poor wages and with no proper career structure.

Three Russians teach the three R's

London Evening Standard, 5 July 2001

The UK has a serious shortage of teachers, particularly in London. Controversially, Gloucester Primary School in Peckham advertised vacancies in newspapers in St Petersburg and today, three female Russian teachers have arrived in London to take up their posts. The government keeps no record of the number of foreign teachers currently in London, but in the last year about 1 200 work permits have been given to teachers seeking work in Britain. Most are from Australia, New Zealand, South Africa and Canada ... there are also thousands more on official extended working holidays. Many are brought over by recruitment agencies who employ them on a daily rate basis. These agencies are now targeting India, China and Jamaica.

Big rise in overseas nurses helps solve recruitment crisis

Nursing Times, 15 August 2001

Nurses from more countries than ever before are arriving in Britain to help resolve the NHS recruitment crisis. In the last year, 8 403 nurses and midwifes who had trained in non-EU countries were registered to work in the UK, a 41 per cent increase on the previous year. The Philippines supplied most, 3 396 compared to 1 052 last year and just 52 in 1998/99. For the time being, Pakistan, Mauritius and the Czech Republic provided new recruits as the NHS widened its search to well over twenty countries. Not all of the new recruits work for the NHS; some work in private nursing homes and it is these that give concern to Unison. Filipino nurses especially are often exploited, abused and bullied. In the worst cases, Unison has helped them do a 'midnight flit' and then find employment in the NHS.

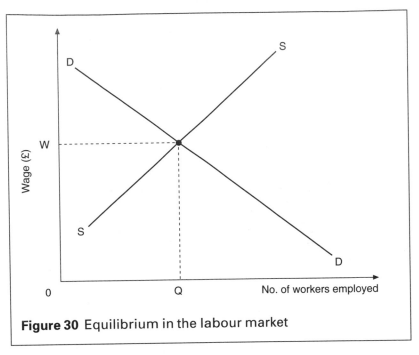

Figure 30 Equilibrium in the labour market

elasticity of supply of nurses (see also Figure 31).

Supply and demand can also be used to explain a fundamental question in the labour market: Why is it that some people are highly paid, whilst others are not? Hospital consultants, for example, get paid more than newly qualified hospital doctors, who in turn get paid more than nurses. The managing director of a tour operator is paid considerably more than a resort representative. The headteacher of a school is paid more than a main grade teacher of the same age and experience.

To answer these questions, economists find it useful to divide earnings into two elements:

- **transfer earnings** – this is the minimum payment necessary to keep labour in its present use
- **economic rent** – any payment to labour which is above transfer earnings.

Both are shown on Figure 32(a). Transfer earnings are indicated by the area under the labour supply curve. Although the equilibrium wage is W, at wages below there are workers who are still willing to offer their services to employers. In fact, at any wage from zero upwards, workers

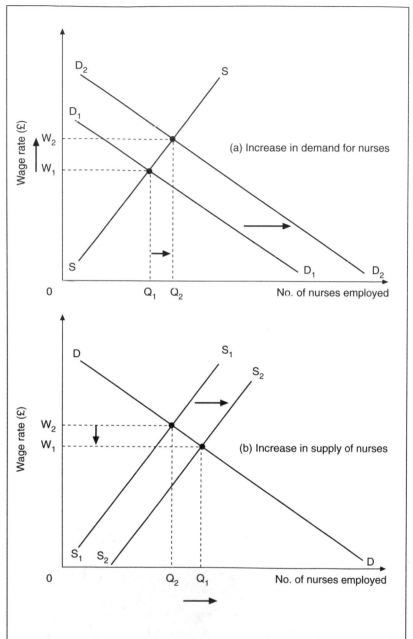

Figure 31 The effects of an increase in demand and supply of nurses

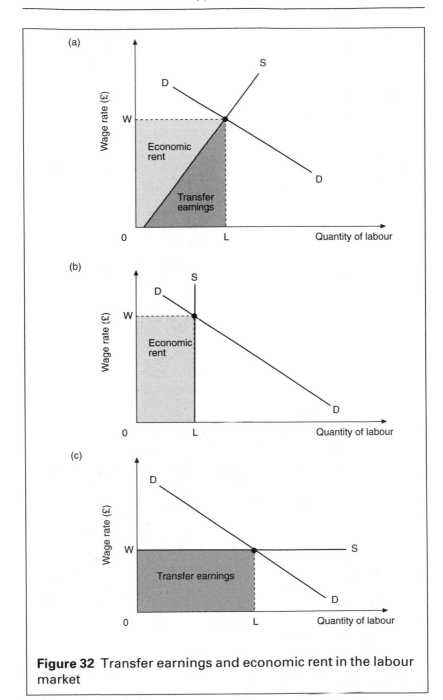

Figure 32 Transfer earnings and economic rent in the labour market

will join the labour market until, at wage W, where the market clears, L supply is available. For those willing to work for less than W, any wages they get over and above what they will accept is their economic rent.

Different workers therefore receive different amounts of transfer earnings and economic rent even in the same job. Returning to nurses, some are willing to work for a low wage below the market equilibrium. These nurses have low transfer earnings and some economic rent. Other nurses may only be induced into employment by the equilibrium wage – in such cases they have no economic rent.

The most highly paid workers such as company bosses and Premier League soccer players have a scarce talent. Their labour supply curve is highly inelastic and in the case of really high earners consists largely of economic rent. In contrast, many workers doing menial jobs (office cleaners for example) have a completely elastic supply. Their earnings consist entirely of transfer earnings: employers can hire all the labour they need at the market wage. These contrasting situations are shown in Figures 32(b) and (c).

The money market

In theory, the interest rate in an economy is like any other price – it is determined by the supply and demand, in this case, for money. This is in essence the Keynesian view. Any change therefore in the conditions of demand and supply will result in the interest rate adjusting to balance these forces in the market.

There are many interest rates in the complex financial markets of the global economy. From the UK's standpoint, the most important one is the base rate which is set by the Monetary Policy Committee of the Bank of England. This team of experts meets monthly to make decisions on short-term interest rates in order to deliver price stability in line with a 2.5 per cent target for RPIX, which has been given to them by the Chancellor of the Exchequer. Another important interest rate is that set by the European Central Bank as the base rate for euro zone members. All specific interest rates follow from these.

The rate of interest is very important since:

- it is the reward for savers who are prepared to part with their money and provide deposits for commercial banks
- it is the cost of borrowing money as paid by individuals and businesses to fund personal and corporate loans
- it determines the value of an asset, such as a bond, which produces a given income stream – when the rate of interest falls, the value of an asset bond will rise, and vice versa.

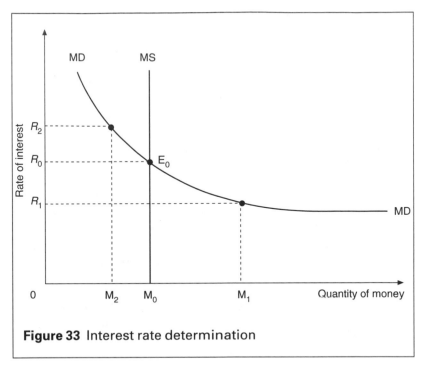

Figure 33 Interest rate determination

Figure 33 shows how the equilibrium interest rate is determined. The two determinants are the **money supply** and **money demand**.

- *The money supply*. This is determined by the government or central bank in an economy. In the short term it remains fixed – this is indicated by the vertical supply curve in Figure 33.
- *The money demand*. There are many reasons why people demand money. The Keynesian liquidity preference theory emphasises that an important influence on how much money people demand is the rate of interest, which is the opportunity cost of holding money. A rise in interest rates will discourage people from holding money. They will instead put money into saving accounts or shares or use it to buy government bonds. These factors result in a downward-sloping demand curve for money.

Returning to Figure 33, equilibrium is at E_0, where the supply and demand for money are M_0, resulting in an interest rate of R_0. If the interest rate is R_1, there will be an excess demand for money of M_0M_1. Bonds will now be offered for sale on the money market in order to increase money holdings in banks. This will result in a fall in bond prices, whilst increasing interest rates up to R_0, where once again there will be equilibrium. In contrast, if the interest rate is R_2, there will be an excess supply of money of $M_2 M_0$. Bonds will now be demanded by people holding excess money reserves. This in turn will force the rate of interest down until it reaches its equilibrium position at R_0.

An increase in the money supply by a central bank will shift the money supply from MS to MS_1 (see Figure 34(a)). This can be done in various ways, for example by buying government bonds through **open market operations**. Consequently, the rate of interest falls to R_1. This fall occurs in order to induce people to hold the additional money that has been created. The lower interest rate reduces the cost of borrowing and the returns for savers. The outcome is that consumers buy more goods, and borrow more money to buy new houses, and firms increase the amount of new factories and equipment that they are funding from borrowed capital. For all of

Japan's economic nightmare

Japan has returned to zero interest rates in a desperate move to stave off recession and a deflationary spiral. The Prime Minister, Yoshino Mori, said that he believed the interest rate cut from 0.15 per cent would have a positive effect on the Japanese economy. His optimism was amid worrying signs that the economy is failing to pull out of a ten-year slump.

Economists fear that the latest interest rate cut can do little to help Japan's fundamental problem ... many people have deserted the banking system. Rather than spend the money they have earned or withdrawn, most are keeping the money at home. About the only market that is booming is that in the sale of home safes! In an economy characterized by falling prices, consumers have learned to wait until goods get cheaper. Others fear for the future preferring to hoard their cash for a rainy day rather than spend it now.

Prices in Japan are falling. There are discounts everywhere. McDonalds sparked a fast food price war with its half-price hamburgers; the Matsuya chain has slashed the price of its gyudon, a beef-topped rice dish; sushi is now eaten more as a fast food; discount retailers and second-hand shops are also doing well. For the last two years, the overall rate of inflation has been negative.

Government economists fear that the economy is caught in a vicious deflationary spiral in which low prices bring companies to their knees, creating unemployment and a further lowering of prices. Their view is that the economy is well and truly stuck in the so-called 'liquidity trap'.

Adapted from *The Singapore Sunday Times*, 3 June 2001

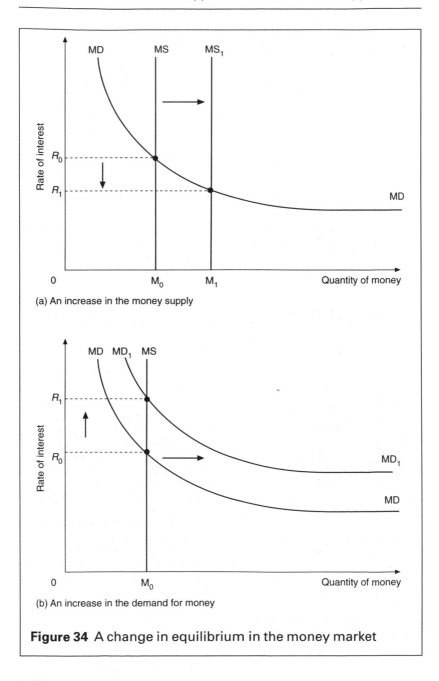

(a) An increase in the money supply

(b) An increase in the demand for money

Figure 34 A change in equilibrium in the money market

these reasons, aggregate demand in the economy increases. Lower interest rates therefore can be the trigger needed by an economy seeking to move out of recession.

Under certain circumstances this may not happen (as in Japan). Here, an economy is in the liquidity trap when, despite low interest rates, speculators are not prepared to take the risks that are necessary to take the economy out of recession. They hold money in this way because they expect bond prices to fall yet again in the future.

An increase in the demand for money is shown on Figure 34(b) by a shift to the right in MD to MD_1. If the rate of inflation increases, then at higher prices, more money is being exchanged every time something is bought and sold. As a result, people will choose to hold a larger quantity of money. This increase in demand affects the equilibrium in the money market. As the money supply remains unchanged, the rate of interest increases to R_1 to discourage the additional demand.

This particular application of supply and demand is interesting, not only for how the money market works, but for how it has an important bearing on the level of aggregate demand in the economy.

Agricultural markets

On the face of it, agricultural markets in developed as well as developing economies appear to meet the conditions for a perfectly competitive market.

- There are a large number of producers. This can be many thousands in the case of large producing economies such as the USA, France, Italy, Spain and UK, and also in the case of most developing economies.
- There are a large number of buyers. This is certainly true if we consider it from a consumer standpoint; it is also true if we look at it from the perspective of wholesalers, food processors, packers and distributors of agricultural products.
- The produce is reasonably homogeneous. Potatoes are potatoes, apples are apples, even allowing for the individual varieties within product groups.
- Producers are **price takers**. No single producer can influence the market price as their output is very small in relation to total production.

- The quality of information in agricultural markets is generally good, with buyers and sellers being well informed about market conditions.
- In principle, farmers make only **normal profits** over the medium to long-term period. If these are not being earned, they can look to diversify what they are doing. If **supernormal profits** are earned, then again in principle, some reallocation of resources will take place and profits will return to normal.

Having said this, some important features of the market should be noted.

Price inelasticity

The demand for agricultural products is relatively price inelastic (see *Chapter Three*). In other words, if the price of food *in general* goes up, people cannot switch to an alternative. We all need food – it has no substitute, although particular agricultural items may well have some substitutes. When prices change, we may consume a little more or a little less of a certain good. In such a situation, where prices fall, the total revenue of producers will fall. This is the more usual case – although there are occasions where, if prices increase, the revenue of farmers will increase. These situations are shown in Figure 35.

Many types of food have close substitutes – examples are chicken and turkey, cabbage and broccoli, or apples and pears. Their price elasticity of demand, though, remains low where they are basic foodstuffs, accounting for a small proportion of consumer incomes.

Income elasticity of demand

The demand for most food items is inelastic with respect to a change in income; and in the case of some food items, the income elasticity of demand is actually negative. This is shown by Table 1 (see page 95).

Rising consumer incomes are 'bad news' for many types of farm producer, both in the UK and elsewhere. As incomes increase, then consumption of all the products and items shown in the left-hand column of Table 1 will decline. Consequently such producers struggle to earn a living in a relatively declining market. Neither is it particularly 'good news' for producers of items in the right-hand column of Table 1. In all cases, demand increases at a lower rate of increase than a change in consumers incomes. The only way in which farm incomes can keep pace with other incomes is for agriculture to become more efficient or if marginal producers leave the market.

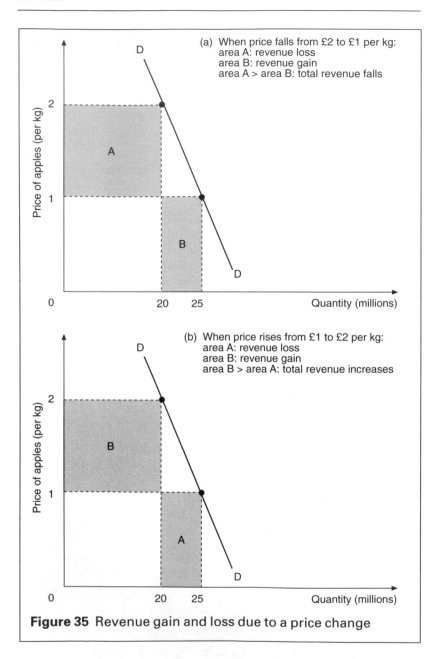

Figure 35 Revenue gain and loss due to a price change

Table 1 Income elasticities of demand for selected food items (in rank order)

Negative elasticity		Positive elasticity	
Sugar and preserves	-0.58	Fruit juice	0.94
Tea	-0.56	Fresh fruit	0.45
Fresh potatoes	-0.48	Coffee	0.23
Margarine	-0.44	Cheese	0.19
Eggs	-0.41	Fresh green vegetables	0.13
Milk	-0.40	Chicken	0.10
Bread	-0.25	Beef	0.08
Lamb	-0.21	Cakes and biscuits	0.02
Processed vegetables	-0.17		
Pork	-0.05		
Butter	-0.04		

Source: Household Food Consumption and Expenditure, ONS, 1998

Uncertain supply

The supply of agricultural products is uncertain owing to the unpredictable nature of production and the problems experienced when farmers try to switch production in response to market forces. Unlike a manufacturing business, a farmer cannot precisely forecast his harvest. Although advanced chemical technology can assist, harvests are affected by rainfall, climate, disease and other natural hazards. The fluctuations in production result in volatile farm incomes. This is shown in Figure 36.

Taking farm products as a whole, an increase in supply over time can be shown by a shift in supply from S_1 to S_2. The increase in demand is much less and is shown by the slight shift of D_1 to D_2. The total effect is clear – market prices will move down from P_1 to P_2, a decline by no means compensated for by the smaller increase in the quantity sold from Q_1 to Q_2. As a consequence, farm incomes are falling. This is particularly the case with basic foodstuffs and products shown on the left-hand side of Table 1. The only exceptions are products where demand is actually increasing, for example exotic fruit and vegetables and organically produced items.

In practice not all farmers can respond to pressures from the market owing to the nature of their land and where they operate. Even where they can respond, it takes time to grow different crops or rear different animals. There is a time lag between a farmer planning to change

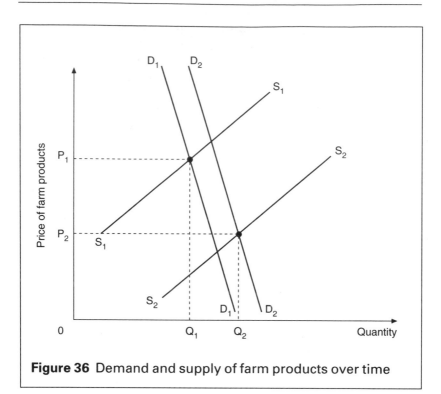

Figure 36 Demand and supply of farm products over time

production and these products reaching the market – and this in itself can result in further, quite violent, price fluctuations.

An alternative approach that could be used is one where producers form a *cartel* and agree to a **buffer stock scheme** in order to reduce price fluctuations. An **intervention price** is agreed within the group, and if the market price falls below this, the cartel will purchase stocks until price reaches the intervention level. If prices rise above the intervention level, stocks will be released on to the market, resulting in a fall in price to the intervention level. The effectiveness of such schemes depends on the resources available to fund as well as manage the organization's attempts to control the market.

The Daily Telegraph article at the beginning of *Chapter Four* showed an interesting and unusual case of coffee production. Table 1 on the previous page indicated a positive income elasticity of demand for coffee of 0.23 for household coffee consumption in the UK. A more detailed analysis of this market will show that as incomes increase then the demand for more expensive coffee, and less instant coffee, has increased. This experience is also repeated in other developed economies. It is therefore very surprising to find that the world price of coffee fell by about thirty per cent between 2000 and 2001, a continuation of what has been a long-term trend in this particular market. The social and economic effects on Colombian producers have been devastating.

The workings of the coffee market have never been easy to explain. The fall in raw bean prices of late seems to be largely due to a rise in the number of producers and output. Vietnam especially has emerged as a major supplier, although its crops tend to be of modest quality. The power of multinational corporations in this market has also had a bearing on lowering prices, despite some of their stated intentions to give a 'fair' price to their suppliers.

The housing market

Our final example, that of the housing market, has certain pecularities yet displays many of the operational features described so far in this chapter.

A house or flat is simply somewhere to live and, in principle, prices should be determined by supply and demand. To some degree this is the case – but the market is complicated by the fact that increasingly, because of rising pries, a house is seen as an asset which gains in value over time. Also, with multiple house ownership, its value as an asset is further reinforced through housing becoming a form of income to some owners, speculators and developers.

The housing market has certain important characteristics.

*   Supply is fixed in the short term. It is rather more elastic in the long term, but there is by no means a free market, owing to planning restrictions, for example. Supply is inflexible and not able to respond to changes in demand in the same way as in most other markets.
*   The market is very clearly divided up into regional sub-markets. If housing is in short supply in Essex, it is no good saying to a prospective buyer that there is good availability in Durham. Within reason, people need to be realistic in relation to where they live and work.
*   Housing has a positive income elasticity of demand. Whether it is a normal or luxury good really depends upon a consumers income. For most people, a house is something that they buy when their income increases. It can become a luxury good when a certain level of income is achieved and the house becomes a good of ostentation, way above what is necessary for day-to-day living.
*   The decision to purchase a house is a long-term one for most

consumers. It requires careful thought and forward planning, and usually requires a capital down-payment prior to purchase. The operation of the market as a consequence is likely to be affected by the confidence that potential consumers have in the market. For example, when consumer confidence is high, owing to the positive state of the macro-economy, demand will be high; in contrast, when the economy is moving into recession, confidence suffers and demand is likely to be restricted.

- Given that many house purchasers need to borrow money, the demand for housing is affected by interest rates. Low interest rates (as we have seen in the UK since 1999) stimulate demand. They mean lower monthly mortgage repayments, so reducing the real amount of the debt.

A combination of many of the above characteristics has served to increase the demand for housing in the UK since 1996, causing average prices to rise well ahead of the rate of inflation. The effect of this is analysed in Figure 37.

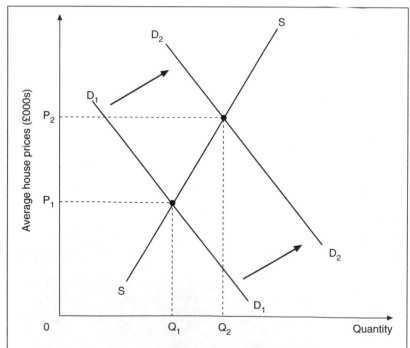

Figure 37 The effects of an increase in demand on the housing market

As the diagram shows, the supply of housing is inelastic. An increase in demand, due say to a rise in incomes or a fall in interest rates or a combination of any of the reasons described above, will result in a sharp increase in prices, with only a small increase in the quantity that is being bought and sold. The more inelastic is supply, and the more inelastic is demand, then the greater will be the increase in prices.

Increasingly, the demand for housing in recent years has become more price inelastic. First-time buyers realize that when interest rates are low it is cheaper to buy than it is to rent, and in so doing they are beginning to grow an asset for the future. Bearing this in mind, some economists argue that the demand curve for housing is actually upward-sloping to a particular price level, indicative of the ever-increasing demand for cheaper housing at a time when supply remains severely restricted.

So much for the theory that underpins the housing market. From an applied perspective, the following key themes can be identified.

The stock or supply of dwellings (that is, flats as well as houses) has increased by two-thirds since 1961 and now stands at around twenty-five million units. This is largely indicative of a changing population structure; there are now an increased number of single-person households than in 1961 and very few households share a dwelling unit with another household. This must not be confused with multi-occupation, which has increased, and is a situation whereby a former single dwelling is split up into two or more units. These trends are projected to continue in the future.

The number of new house-building completions has been very stable at around 200 000 per annum over the past twenty years or so. The vast proportion of this is provided by the private sector. Local authorities now have a very minimal role, although registered housing associations and charities build between twenty and thirty thousand units a year.

Owner-occupation (that is, where households actually buy or borrow to buy their dwelling) has increased steadily from around 45 per cent in 1961 to almost 70 per in 2001. An important factor over the past twenty years or so has been the legislation that has allowed public-sector tenants to buy their homes.

In January 2002, the average dwelling price in England and Wales reached £100,000, although there were marked regional variations in prices (see *The Daily Telegraph* article). House prices in London have tended to lead the rest of the country. For a detached house, the amount paid by buyers in London was over three times that paid by buyers in Wales. Similarly, a terraced house in London was well over four times the cost of a similar property in the North West.

99

Average house 'breaks £100 000 barrier'

SIMON GOODLEY

The average cost of a UK house rose above £100 000 for the first time last month as confident buyers continued to take advantage of low interest rates.

Year	Average house price
1945	£1 000
1954	£2 000
1970	£5 000
1973	£10 000
1983	£25 000
1988	£50 000
1999	£75 000
2002	£1000 000

Source: BSDA and Halifax

House prices increased by 1.6 per cent in January, giving an annual inflation rate of 16.8 per cent, the largest boost since the 18.1 per cent recorded in the boom of 1989. The monthly rate of growth, however, slowed after a 2.8 per cent increase in December, according to Halifax's house price index.

The figures were stronger than a similar report produced by rival lender Nationwide, which said that house price inflation slowed to just 0.2 per cent in January from 1.9 per cent in December.

The Halifax said the average cost of a UK home was now £100 400, which could buy properties from a one-bedroom flat in London to a four-bedroom executive home in County Down, Northern Ireland.

It added that the continued increase in prices reflected a bounce back in confidence from the lows seen in the aftermath of September 11.

Martin Ellis, group economist at Halifax, said: 'Mortgage payments are a smaller proportion of people's income than at any time in the past twenty years'. He added that a mortgage for a typical first-time buyer accounts for about 13 per cent of gross income, compared with a twenty-year average of 24 per cent and a peak of 41 per cent in March 1990.

The report also said the price increases were due to supply shortages in the market: new home building has fallen to a 77-year low. In 2001, 162 000 new homes were built, compared with a peak of 413 000 in 1968.

A spokesman said: 'The country needs 200 000 new homes annually to keep pace with the growth in households. With just over 160 000 being built, we have a serious problem.'

Economists said that the price news would make the Bank of England's monetary policy committee even more reluctant to cut rates. A UK economist at investment bank Merrill Lynch said: 'We expect unemployment to rise this year, but that is not what affects house prices. Interest rates will remain low until the second half of the year. We expect house prices to rise around eight per cent this year.'

Halifax added that it expects that higher unemployment later this year will knock confidence, causing the housing market to 'ease back', although prices will still rise.

Adapted from *The Daily Telegraph*, 25 January 2002

Average prices since 1995 have accelerated at well above the rate of inflation owing to low interest rates and a strong macro-economy. Currently the expectation is that this growth will slow down owing to more uncertain economic prospects, the continued fall in manufacturing employment, and restraints on earnings.

Conclusion

This chapter has given a wide range of examples of 'markets in action'. In all cases, the basic economics of markets can be applied – price is determined by the combined forces of demand and supply – although each individual market has its own peculiar characteristics. A knowledge of these characteristics is therefore very important when analysing each market situation.

KEY WORDS

Euro	Appreciation
Labour market	Freely floating
Wages	Derived demand
Money market	Marginal revenue product
Rate of interest	Transfer earnings
Commodity markets	Economic rent
Housing market	Money supply
Foreign exchange market	Money demand
Imports	Open market operations
Exports	Price takers
International tourism	Normal profits
Foreign direct investment	Supernormal profits
Exchange rate	Buffer stock scheme
Depreciation	Intervention price

Further reading

Bamford, C. (ed.), Chapter 1 in *Transport Economics*, 3rd edn, Heinemann Educational, 2001.

Grant, S. and Vidler, C., Part 1, Units 28 and 30, and part 2, Units 5, 14 and 23 in *Economics in Context*, Heinemann Educational, 2000.

Hale, G., Chapters 1 and 2 in *Labour Markets*, Heinemann Educational, 2001.

Russell, M. and Heathfield, D., Chapter 6 in *Inflation and UK Monetary Policy*, 3rd edn, Heinemann Educational, 1999.

Useful websites
- Labour market: www.statistics.gov.uk
  Click on economy; Search for labour market.
- Housing market: www.houseweb.co.uk

Essay topics
1. (a) Explain how the value of the pound sterling is determined.
   [20 marks]
   (b) Discuss four cases of a fall in the value of the pound.
   [12 marks]
2. Discuss why barristers are paid more than bar staff.   [20 marks]

Data response question
This task is based on a question set by Edexcel in January 2001. Read the piece below, which is adapted from 'Boom in house prices set to continue' by Lea Paterson, published in *The Times* on 5 January 2000. Then answer the questions that follow.

House price boom

After allowing for inflation, UK house prices rose by fifteen per cent in 1999. All the signs are that house prices are set for further large increases, despite recent increases in interest rates.

In any case, the Bank of England changes only short-term interest rates, which affect borrowing costs for those homeowners on variable rate mortgages. The price of fixed-rate mortgages, held by a sizeable number of homeowners, is not affected in the short term.

Other factors that might reduce future demand are the abolition of mortgage interest tax relief (MIRAS) and the steady decline of the number 20 to 29-year old housebuyers – traditionally the age group most likely to plunge into the housing market. However, tax relief has been worth relatively little to borrowers in recent years, and the decline in the number of 20 to 29-year old housebuyers is most likely to be offset by other population factors.

From an historical perspective, it is real incomes, not interest rates or tax incentives, that have had most impact on the housing market. With economic growth set to rise further this year, real incomes are likely to grow strongly. City forecasters expect a rise of 3.5 per cent, which, if coupled with a 3 per cent rise in 1999, will make the average household substantially better off. Add to this the fact that affordability remains good – that is, housing is cheap relative to incomes – and conditions look set for further sharp house price rises. This all suggests that the UK property boom has some way to go. Apart from some external shock – such as a prolonged period of stock market fluctuations – all looks set fair for the UK economy. First-time buyers may be well advised to buy now, while they still can.

1. Using a supply and demand diagram, analyse why 'house prices are set for further large increases'. [4 marks]

2. (a) Explain the term 'income elasticity of demand'. [2 marks]
    (b) What does the passage suggest about the income elasticity of demand for house purchase? [2 marks]

3. Examine the likely significance of *two* factors mentioned in the passage that might 'reduce future housing demand'. [6 marks]

4. (a) Identify *two* reasons why 'first-time buyers may be well advised to buy now, while they still can'. [2 marks]
    (b) Discuss the importance to first-time buyers of the two reasons you have identified. [4 marks]

Chapter Seven

Markets and market structures

'The Competition Commission are satisfied that the [supermarket]
industry is currently broadly competitive and that overall excessive
prices are not being charged ... a competitive market is the best way of
securing a good deal for the consumer'
Competition Commission, 2000

An important assumption in the analyses in *Chapters One* to *Six* has
been that markets operate freely, with the respective forces of demand
and supply determining the market price and the quantity that is
purchased and produced. The so-called 'invisible hand', as Adam Smith
called it, is assumed to be a self-regulating process through which the
fundamental economic problem is resolved. In some of the applications
given in the last chapter, this basically runs true; in many markets,
though, the assumptions that economists make do not hold true.
Consequently, markets do not always operate in the ways that we have
described.

The model of perfect competition (or total competition as it is
sometimes called) consists of many firms and can be described as a
market structure in which firms have no power over the price charged
for their product. In other words, they are **price takers**, accepting the
price set by the market. This is an essential requirement for markets to
operate freely. Other assumptions for competitive markets are
examined below.

Assumptions for competitive markets

Five particular assumptions are made.

- *There are many purchasers or consumers of a product.* The
  significance of this is that single purchasers cannot influence the
  market price by their actions in the market.
- *Many firms are present.* Typically each firm is small, there are many
  of them, and no single firm can affect the market supply curve by
  actions, say, in restricting output. It follows that the firm is not only
  a price taker but that its demand curve is perfectly elastic. Firms will
  be able to sell all they can produce at the market-clearing price. At
  any other price above the equilibrium price, they will sell little; there
  is no point in them selling below this price.

- *There is perfect information.* Firms and purchasers are aware of the price that is set by the market. Moreover, if, for example, a firm sets a price above this clearing price, purchasers will transfer their consumption to the products of another firm as they have perfect information about prices in the market. Additionally, firms will know what prices are being set by all other producers.
- *Firms produce identical or homogenous products.* This is further reason why the demand curve is perfectly elastic. For purchasers, it does not matter at all from which firm they buy their products. All are alike and all are available at the same price.
- *There is freedom of entry and exit.* This means that any firm that wishes to produce in the market can do so. There are no costs of entry and no barriers to prevent firms from producing. Firms are also free to leave the market and will incur no additional costs when they do so. The outcome of this is that, in the long run, all firms will earn **normal profits**. These can be defined as the profit necessary to the firm operating in an industry in the long run. They can be seen therefore as a legitimate cost of production.

Markets in reality

In considering how markets actually operate, two factors have particular significance.

- *Barriers to entry.* These are any obstacles that prevent new firms from entering an industry. Where present, they give firms market power in that decisions can be made by existing firms without the risk of losing market share or their price being challenged by new firms entering a market. Barriers to entry take a variety of forms – such as the cost of setting up in an industry, branding that can make it difficult for new entrants to make an impact, legal barriers and patents, and the benefits of economies of scale for established large producers. The strength of barriers to entry therefore determines the power that existing producers have in a market.
- *The number of firms.* In reality, not many markets have the large number of price takers that are necessary for perfect competition. Increasingly, most markets are dominated by a small number of large firms to the extent that they are able to protect their market share from potential entrants.

Figure 38 shows the so-called **spectrum of competition**. This indicates the range of models of market structure that have been developed by economists to benchmark or act as a framework for real-world competitive markets.

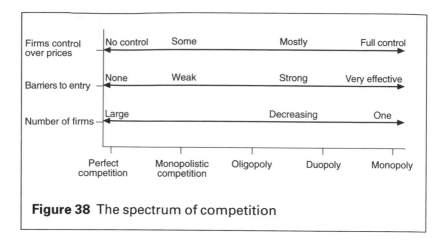

Figure 38 The spectrum of competition

A detailed analysis of all of these market structures can be found in *Business Economics* by A. Griffiths and S. Ison (Heinemann Educational, 2001).

A brief commentary on the implications of particular market structures for the operation of the market is appropriate at this stage. Figure 38 shows the spectrum of competition:

- As stated above, the principles of the free market prevail in a perfectly competitive market. Prices are determined by the twin forces of demand and supply and the market clears where they are in equilibrium.

- With **monopolistic competition**, the goods and services that are produced are differentiated, not homogeneous. Each firm makes products that are slightly different from those of their competitors. The demand for products, though, is responsive to price as all products have close substitutes. Individual firms are price makers, rather than price takers.

- A key feature of **oligopoly** is the interdependence of firms – the actions of one firm are likely to provoke a reaction or counter-action from rivals. **Price rigidity**, illustrated by a kinked demand curve, is another key feature. Prices tend to be stable over time; firms compete more in terms of their products and the benefits they can provide to customers.

- A **duopoly** is where there are just two firms in an industry. In theory they have equal market shares, identical cost structures and their products are not differentiated. Their prices are identical.

- A **monopoly** in the strictest sense is a market with just one firm. This firm is a **price maker**, there are high barriers to entry, and no close substitutes are available.

As we move along the spectrum of competition, the ability of firms to influence the market increases. It is particularly strong in the cases of duopoly and monopoly where firms set their own prices, the quantity demanded then being determined by just how much consumers are prepared to pay at that price. In reality, as we shall show below, oligopolies are very powerful in the ways in which they exert pressures on the market, particularly involving **non-price competition**.

A relatively recent approach to the description of markets is the notion of **contestability**. Referring back to the start of this section, a contestable market is one in which:

- there is free entry (and exit) in the market – potential entrants are therefore at no disadvantage compared with firms already operating in a particular market
- the number and size of firms is irrelevant since only normal profits are being earned in the long run.

This practical notion of markets, developed by the US economist Baumol, is an important and realistic benchmark by which actual market structures can be judged. In many respects it is a more appropriate barometer of competition than the perfect-competition model in the complex economies of the twenty-first century. Further details on its relevance in transport markets is in Chapter 5 of *Transport Economics* by C. G. Bamford (Heinemann Educational, 2000).

Identifying market power

There are various approaches to estimating the extent to which a market may be controlled by the firms that operate within it. A few such indicators will now be described.

One of the best measures used by economists is that of a **concentration ratio**. This is a measure of the percentage of sales in a market that accrue to the three, five or seven largest firms. The bigger this percentage, the closer the industry is to the right-hand side of the spectrum of competition shown in Figure 38. Some of the highest five-firm concentration ratios in the UK are in industry groups such as vehicle manufacturing, pharmaceuticals, cement, chocolate and sugar confectionery, brewing, grocery retailing, banking, and package holidays. Firms in such industries are invariably powerful forces in the markets where they operate.

The number of firms in an industry is another measure. The bigger the total, the closer the industry is towards a perfect market. This measure can be somewhat misleading, as there could be a small number of large firms dominating a market but hundreds of smaller firms also present. Grocery retailing is a particularly good example of this, as too is brewing.

The extent of barriers to entry can also be important in determining market power. Looking at how difficult it is for new firms to set up in an industry can give a good indication of the power that existing firms have in an industry.

Economies of scale especially can make it very difficult for new firms to enter a market. A good example here is the seemingly contestable market for local bus services in the UK. New firms are finding it increasingly difficult to compete with the large powerful oligopolists that now dominate the market. Market entry is becoming increasingly problematic, with vast sums of capital now being needed if new firms wish to run services in most of our towns and cities.

Case study: supermarkets in the UK

The big supermarkets in the UK are a very good example of an oligopoly industry. As Table 2 indicates, the five-firm concentration ratio in 2001 was estimated to be about 50 per cent of grocery sales. This ratio has increased over the past twenty years or so, making the large supermarket groups very powerful players in their market.

Table 2 UK supermarket market share in 2001

	Market share percentage
Tesco	16.5
Sainsbury's	11.6
Asda	9.6
Safeway	7.5
Somerfield/Kwik Save	4.7

Note: Includes ambient, fresh, chilled and frozen goods plus alcoholic drink and tobacco sales.
Source: Institute of Grocery Distribution, 2002

Their power comes in many forms, such as:

- benefits from economies of scale in purchasing
- central purchasing and distribution systems
- own-label products which are designed to promote customer loyalty
- stipulating prices with their dedicated suppliers such as farmers and food manufacturers
- pricing basic goods at below cost in order to attract customers and force out rivals
- full control over their supply chains
- extended opening hours and diversification with local retailing.

A common perception is that consumers are being 'ripped off' by the large supermarkets, their profits are excessive compared with similar firms in the rest of the EU and that through their activities thousands of small corner shops have been forced out of business.

It was against this background that, after a two-year investigation, the

---

'Rip-off Britain' – no case to answer

The outcome of a £20 million inquiry by the Competition Commission cleared the big supermarket chains of allegations that they were profiteering at the public's expense. The investigation was ordered as a result of claims that

- the profit margins of UK supermarkets was typically five–six per cent, compared with much lower margins in France and Germany
- there were substantial barriers to entry facing new competitors
- the prices of branded items were often set to match rather than undercut the prices of competitors
- savings from bulk buying and seasonal price reductions were not being passed on to customers
- customers in some parts of the country were faced with little choice of retail supermarket.

The Competition Commission investigated all of these claims and, overall, found little cause for concern except for:

- the selling of particular lines at well below cost constituted unfair competition from the viewpoint of smaller retailers
- local monopolies do push up the bills of customers who are a captive market.

Their main recommendation was that a new code of practice should be introduced to police the relationship between suppliers – particularly farmers – and the stores.

The farmer living in fear

Farmer Robert Cauldwell says he has seen colleagues financially ruined by the big stores. 'Farmers are living in fear of the supermarkets and I do not think much is going to change,' he said as the Competition Commission's verdict left him deeply dismayed.

Quite often, growers and farmers have had to agree to sell their produce at below cost price just to ensure they keep the contract. That cannot be fair. It is particularly troubling when you compare the low prices we get with the amount the consumer has to pay. All we want is a fair share of the retail price.'

The Daily Mail, 11 October 2000

Competition Commission controversially concluded in October 2000 that the large supermarkets *were* operating in the general interest of consumers and that there was a competitive market which was the best way to secure a good deal for consumers (see the box 'Rip-off Britain').

Not all would agree with this conclusion. Farmers especially live in fear of the power of the large supermarket chains, and the livelihoods of many small shopkeepers have been badly affected (see the extracts from the *Daily Mail* and *The Daily Telegraph*).

English-born Asians spurn long hours of family business

Narendra Patel was preparing to take his A levels in Britain when he discovered that his dream of becoming a doctor would never be fulfilled. His family were given just 72 hours to leave their native Uganda. That was in 1972. They arrived in Britain as penniless refugees, a far cry from their middle class status in their home country.

Like many others, the Patel's route to renewed prosperity was via the corner shop. Narendra Patel bought his first shop in Wembley in 1976 and by 1989 had eight shops. He now retains just one shop.

Over the past decade, the number of such small shops has fallen from 15 000 to about 11 500. Second-generation Asians do not want to work long hours – most prefer to seek a professional career – but the Patels, like many others have seen their business suffer at the hands of new chains such as Tesco Metro, which offer late-night convenience shopping, a wider product range and prices which are very 'competitive'.

Adapted from *The Daily Telegraph*, 5 January 2002

Licence awards leave Royal Mail facing death by a thousand cuts

Are we about to witness the death, by a thousand cuts, of the Royal Mail?

Yesterday, Hays the distribution and logistics company, was awarded the first licence to operate against Royal Mail. But no sooner had the regulator signed off Hays' licence to operate business services in London, Edinburgh and Manchester than two other would-be rivals popped up.

UK Mail, a division of Business Post, is applying for permission to offer a service to about 5 000 business customers in Birmingham, Bristol, Edinburgh, Leeds, Leicester, Liverpool, London, Manchester and the Thames Valley.

The other rival is tabling a more inno-vative, controversial proposal. Deya, a small Wokingham-based distribution company, is offering a strike-breaking service. It wants to deliver council tax bills and utility bills if services are hit by industrial action. The company, which delivers Yellow Pages, BT telephone directories and other commercial items, devised the plan after being approached by a utility more than five years ago in the aftermath of the Post Office's national strike. Postcomm has already said that it is minded to grant a short-term licence.

As the rivals circle (not forgetting TNT of course), the Royal Mail is looking at its own shake-up to prepare its business for life in an interesting competitive market.

Adapted from *The Times*, 18 September 2001

Case study: Postal services in the UK

At present, Consignia (Royal Mail Group plc from 2003) has a monopoly over the collection of mail that is posted through letter boxes the length and breadth of the UK. Its universal postal obligation requires it to charge the same price per item that goes from one end of the country to the other as for mail which travels just a short distance. Consignia finds its business under threat due to:

- sustained losses in recent years
- the need to improve efficiency, cut back on restrictive practices, and reduce staffing levels
- deregulation, which will introduce competition into the market
- a fall in demand for its core business owing to fewer letters being written, increased mobile telephone ownership, and the widespread use of e-mail, especially for business communications.

The industry's regulator, Postcomm, has been charged with opening the market to competition, whilst controlling prices and the quality of services provided. Its first act has been to grant licences to three new operators (see *The Times* article). Although as yet these are not set to radically undermine Consignia's core business, the message to the former state monopoly is very clear: Postcomm is determined that there will be increasing competition in this once-protected market.

In May 2002, after intensive lobbying from the Government, trade unions and Consignia, Postcomm unveiled a phased programme of opening up the postal market to full competition by April 2007. There are three important stages:

• January 2003 – competitors will be able to bid to deliver bulk mail above 4000 items. This will include mailshots from insurance and banking providers, bills from gas, electricity and water companies and from local authorities.

• April 2005 – small bulk mail deliveries will be opened up to competition.

• April 2007 – the rest of Consignia's monopoly will be subject to competition. Principally, this will involve the removal of Consignia's monopoly for delivering letters of less than 100g weight.

The way is now clear for rival postal operators such as Business Post, TNT and the Dutch post Office TPG to apply for licences to compete in these business sectors. As with other privatisations (gas, electricity, telephones and railways), a key issue that still has to be resolved is the price that the regulator will set for access to the Royal Mail's so-called 'final mile' network. The intention is that Royal Mail postal staff will deliver the mail posted through the networks of their competitors. It is clearly uneconomic for rival companies to have their own dedicated delivery staff. This charge will ultimately determine just how much competition there will be in the postal market.

Case Study – Brewing Industry

The brewing industry in a simple sense is concerned with the production of beer and other alcoholic drinks. Through growth, acquisitions and diversification, the main brewing companies are now involved in a much wider range of activities, including restaurants, hotels and leisure facilities. The emergence of powerful companies in what is now a high concentration market has much in common with the UK grocery market (see the case study on page 108) but unlike supermarkets, the activities of the brewing companies have been subject to very important regulation and control from the Competition Commission and the Office of Fair Trading. The ways in which brewing companies operate appears to match what economists have to say about markets where there is little competition.

Traditionally, through the tied house system, brewing companies were able to control the sale of their own products in licensed premises. They were also able to prohibit the sale of competitor's products and regulate prices. In 1989, these controversial activities were the subject of a report from the Monopolies and Mergers Commission which

- required brewers to own no more than 2000 public houses
- eliminated the tied house arrangements
- required public houses to buy at least one brand of beer from a brewer other than their normal supplier.

The MMC's intention was to increase competition in the market and increase consumer choice and value. The changes in ownership since 1989 have been remarkable (see Table 3). These have come about through the directives of the government's regulatory bodies and other ownership changes that have seen non-UK companies enter the market.

Table 3 Market Shares in UK Beer Market, 1989–2001

1989		1996		2001	
Bass	22%	Scottish Courage	31%	Scottish Courage	25%
Allied-Lyons	14%	Bass	23%	Interbrew	22%
Grand Met.	15%	Carlsberg Tetley	16%	Coors (Carling)	20%
Whitbread	13%	Whitbread	14%	Carlsberg Tetley	18%
Scottish and Newcastle	11%	Others	16%	Others	15%
Courage	10%				
Others	17%				

The Governments concern has been to break down the brewers monopoly mainly through the control they exercised through vertical integration in the market. The 1989 Supply of Beer report from the MMC firmly took the stand that these practices were against the public interest. The outcome is that the brewing companies have had to decide whether to brew or retail beer. Most took the decision to sell off thousands of their public houses to new owners such as Enterprise Inns, Normura International and Punch Group whilst retaining the maximum number allowed by the MMC's directive.

Government intervention has undoubtedly made the brewing

industry more competitive. In particular it has put pressure on retail and wholesale prices in a way that was not the case with the tied house system. Customers have further benefited with product diversification, notably new theme pubs which are targeting particular segments of the market.

As Table 3 indicated, the brewing industry remains highly concentrated, with the Big Four now producing 85 per cent of all beer produced in the UK. Further mergers and acquisitions could well take place subject to government approval. The big brewers are increasingly powerful global businesses, with an emerging portfolio of global brands. They may not now have as much control over their core business – they are nevertheless in a strong position to influence the markets in which they operate.

Conclusion

This final chapter has demonstrated that microeconomic policy seeks to create a situation where seemingly uncompetitive markets remain subject to the competitive forces of demand and supply. This has been an important objective of the work of the Competition Commission in markets such as grocery retailing where the general perception is that large businesses are exerting tremendous control over the natural workings of the market. As we have demonstrated in this book, the free-market mechanism has much to commend it from the point of view of achieving a smooth, natural allocation of resources.

KEY WORDS

Price taker	Price rigidity
Normal profits	Duopoly
Spectrum of competition	Monopoly
Monopolistic competition	Price maker
Oligopoly	Non-price competition

Further reading

Bamford, C. (ed.), Unit 1, section 3 in *Economics for AS*, Cambridge University Press, 2000.

Grant, S. and Vidler, C., Part 3, Unit 12 in *Economics in Context*, Heinemann Educational, 2000.

Griffiths, A. and Ison, S., Chapters 3–8 in *Business Economics*, Heinemann Educational, 2001.

Munday, S., Chapters 3 and 4 in *Markets and Market Failure*, Heinemann Educational, 2000.

Useful website

Competition Commission: www.competition-commission.org.uk

Essay topics

1. (a) Distinguish between perfect competition and monopoly.

      [10 marks]

   (b) Explain the effect that the existence of barriers to entry is likely to have on a market. [10 marks]

2. (a) Discuss how the degree of competition existing in a market can be assessed. [10 marks]

   (b) Explain how the level of competition in a market influences the price elasticity of demand for a firm's product. [10 marks]

Data response question

This task is based on a question set by OCR in June 2001. Read the piece below, and study Table A (adapted from *The Daily Telegraph*, 11 March 2000) and Table B. Then answer the questions that follow.

Big fish prowl in holiday waters

Last year, eighteen million Britons went on package holidays. Most of these were low- to mid-priced 'sun and sand' packages to the Mediterranean and to Florida with one of the big operators. Until recently, these companies battled away at selling holidays in this market. Since 1997 though, the 'Big Four' (see Table A) have bought more than two dozen smaller specialist tour operators. Their new owners have quietly taken over without changing the names or the brochures of these companies. Through this take-over strategy, they have increased market share, made it more difficult for others to compete, and moved more up-market in their product range. The effects of all this activity on the profit levels of tour operators remains to be seen. One must also ask whether this means less choice and higher prices for their customers.

The package holiday business is a complex one, which requires the tour operators to secure accommodation and flights often twelve–eighteen months ahead of departure. Thereafter, matching this supply with demand from holidaymakers takes place via the market mechanism. Peak-period prices, usually during school holidays, are much higher than the equivalent off-peak package. Equally, if customers want choice then they must book early, otherwise they take a risk that the holiday of their dreams will not be available at the last minute at a reduced price.

Table B shows some estimated elasticities of demand for three typical package holidays.

Table A The Big Four: Who owns what?

- **Thomson**
  Airline Britannia
  Travel agents Lunn Poly and others
  Tour operators Thomson Holidays, Portland, Crystal, Tropical Places, Austravel, Country Cottages in France, Chez Nous, Something Special, Magic Travel Group, Simply Travel, Spanish Harbour, Headwater
- **Airtours**
  Airline Airtours International
  Travel agents Going Places and others
  Tour operators Airtours, Aspro, Tradewinds, Eurosites, Cresta, Manos, Bridge Travel, Jetset, Panorama, Direct Holidays, Swiss Travel Service
- **First Choice**
  Airline Air 2000
  Travel agents Travel Choice and others
  Tour operators First Choice, Sovereign, 2wentys, Meon, Sunsail, Eclipse, Unijet, Hayes & Jarvis
- **Thomas Cook**
  Airline Flying Colours and Caledonian – to be rebranded as JMC
  Travel agents Thomas Cook
  Tour operators JMC, Club 18–30, Neilson, Time Off, Thomas Cook Holidays

Table B Elasticity of demand estimates

Package holiday type	Price elasticity of demand		Income elasticity of demand
	Peak	Off-peak	
Self-catering to Ibiza	−0.6	−1.2	−1.0
Fly-drive to Florida	−0.8	−1.4	1.6
Villa holiday to Portugal	−0.4	−0.8	2.4

1. State and give examples of *three* different factors of production needed to produce a package holiday. [6 marks]

2. (a) Define elasticity of supply. [2 marks]
   (b) Using the information in the first sentence of the second paragraph, would you expect the elasticity of supply for package holidays to be elastic or inelastic? Justify your answer. [3 marks]

3. (a) Explain what is meant by consumer surplus. [2 marks]
   (b) With the aid of a diagram, explain how 'higher prices for their customers' would affect consumer surplus. [4 marks]

4. With reference to Table B, use diagrams to analyse how an increase in the incomes of package holiday takers might affect their demand for (i) self-catering holidays in Ibiza, and (ii) villa holidays in Portugal. [6 marks]

5. (a) State and describe *two* characteristics of an oligopoly. [4 marks]
   (b) To what extent does the packaged holiday market match these characteristics? [8 marks]

6. Discuss how the information in Table B could be used by a tour operator. [10 marks]

Data response question

This task is based on a question set by Edexcel in June 2002. Read the piece below and then answer the questions that follow.

The proposed merger between Lloyds TSB Group and Abbey National

The Secretary of State for Trade and Industry asked us to investigate the implications for the public interest of the proposed acquisition of Abbey National plc by Lloyds Group plc.

Lloyds TSB has for many years been one of the four leading clearing banks in the UK, the others being Barclays, HSBC and the Royal Bank of Scotland – National Westminster Bank Group.

Abbey National was in 1989 the first building society to convert from mutual to public limited company (plc) status. Subsequently it has

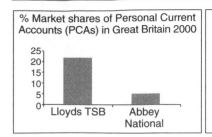

% Market shares of Personal Current Accounts (PCAs) in Great Britain 2000

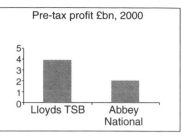

Pre-tax profit £bn, 2000

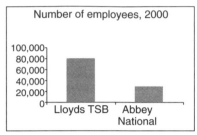

Number of employees, 2000

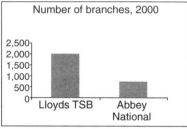

Number of branches, 2000

developed into an organisation offering a full range of banking services.

Personal Current Accounts (PCAs) are the core product in personal banking. They also serve as a 'gateway' through which suppliers can sell other financial products, such as credit cards and personal loans as a result of the relationship established through the PCA. The merger would increase the PCA share of Lloyds TSB, already the market leader, from 22 to 27 per cent and would raise the combined share of the four big banks from 72 to 77 percent.

There are several features of the PCA market which make the market vulnerable to unspoken and unwritten collusion in pricing in ways in which serve the banks' common commercial interest. These features would tend to increase any adverse effects on competition arising from the loss of a significant player.

The entrenched position of the big four banks remains strong. Customers tend to see switching accounts between banks as a difficult and unrewarding process and the rate of switching is very low. Entry by new forms has been limited.

Having reviewed all possibilities we have concluded that prohibiting the merger is the only course of action likely to preserve the public interest.

www.competition-commission.org.uk

1. (a) Identify the market structure of the banking sector. Justify your answer with evidence from the evidence in the passage.
      [4 marks]
   (b) What kind of integration is involved in the proposed acquisition? Explain using evidence from the passage.
      [4 marks]
   (c) What evidence in the data suggests that the proposed merger was eligible for referral to the Competition Commission?
      [4 marks]

2. Analyse why the Personal Current Account (PCA) market might be 'vulnerable to unspoken and unwritten collusion in pricing' (lines 16–17).   [8 marks]

3. Examine possible reasons why in this sector of the economy 'entry by new firms has been limited' (line 22).   [10 marks]

4. Assess the extent to which a reduced number of commercial banks might be against the interests of bank customers.   [10 marks]

Conclusion

The Introduction and the epigraphs at the start of *Chapters One, Two* and *Four* have made reference to economic ideas contained in Adam Smith's *The Wealth of Nations*. Two hundred years on, the basic principles and philosophy of market economics, as put forward by Smith and his successors, remains. The purpose of this book has been to examine this most fundamental aspect of economics both in theory and in terms of its present day applications.

To this end the book is self-contained. In other respects, it is the first stage along the road to economic explanation. From this foundation, other books in the series will provide the means for widening as well as deepening the study of markets. Bearing this in mind, the following general conclusions can be made:

Market economics has stood the test of time. It remains a robust and central part of the study of economics and has considerable relevance today.

Any market can be described in terms of a demand side and a supply side.

Market economics recognizes the respective objectives of consumers and firms. An understanding of these objectives is essential for understanding how each behave in particular market situations.

The beauty of the market is that it is a self-regulating mechanism which can produce an efficient allocation of resources. Consumers and producers will be satisfied with the outcome provided neither has the power to interfere in its operation.

The basic principles of operation of markets can be applied to a wide range of actual market situations.

This is not the end of the story. A full perspective on how markets work has to address why in some cases, markets 'fail'. Here, market forces do not operate as the theory suggests and so governments have to intervene to correct a range of market failures. This important subject is investigated in co-author Stephen Munday's companion text, *Markets and Market Failure*, Heinemann Educational, 2000.

In common with other books in the series, we have sought to demonstrate that economics has a value and relevance outside the classroom. Even in this most basic of areas – markets – economics provides a relevant means of understanding the ever-changing world in which we live and work. If our readers can comprehend this, then we have achieved our objective.

Index

Thorough coverage of topical issues: there's a SEB for every part of your course!

Having seen how good *Markets* is, you might be interested to know about other books in the *Studies in Economics and Business* series. The books in this series are easy-to-understand yet comprehensive making them ideal for AS and A2 students looking for in-depth information on particular topics.

External Influences examines the key outside influences on business. These include the effect of technology, society and politics on business behaviour. Like other books in the series it includes European and global perspectives giving you an international view of Economics and Business.

The Economics of Leisure draws on economic theory to examine trends in the leisure industry. There are plenty of press cuttings and real-life examples helping you relate the theory to everyday life.

External Influences	0 435 33217 1
The Economics of Leisure	0 435 33045 4

There are many more books in the series. Titles include: *The European Union, Business Economics, UK Current Economic Policy, Supply Side Policies, Green Economics,* and *Human Resource Management.*

To order these or to find out about other books in the series call **01865 888068** or visit our website at **www.heinemann.co.uk**

F 999 ADV 08

F975T